The HEALTHY BRAIN Book of SUDOKU Variants

Bastien Vial-Jaime

PUZZLE
WRIGHT
PRESS

New York

PUZZLE WRIGHT PRESS

New York

An Imprint of Sterling Publishing Co., Inc.

PUZZLEWRIGHT PRESS and the distinctive Puzzlewright Press logo
are registered trademarks of Sterling Publishing Co., Inc.

Puzzles and chapter text © 2022 Bastien Vial-Jaime
Introduction © 2022 Sterling Publishing Co., Inc.

ISBN 978-1-4549-4464-5

Distributed in Canada by Sterling Publishing Co., Inc.
C/o Canadian Manda Group, 664 Annette Street
Toronto, Ontario M6S 2C8, Canada
Distributed in the United Kingdom by GMC Distribution Services
Castle Place, 166 High Street, Lewes, East Sussex BN7 1XU, England
Distributed in Australia by NewSouth Books
University of New South Wales, Sydney, NSW 2052, Australia

For information about custom editions, special sales, and premium and corporate purchases,
please contact Sterling Special Sales at specialsales@sterlingpublishing.com.

Manufactured in China

2 4 6 8 10 9 7 5 3 1

sterlingpublishing.com
puzzlewright.com

Cover design by Igor Satanovsky
Cover image: Boy Fahri/Shutterstock.com

CONTENTS

INTRODUCTION

Studies have shown that one of the best ways to keep your mind fit is to keep learning new things, creating fresh neural connections in your brain as you navigate an unfamiliar intellectual landscape. And if you're a puzzle lover, that probably sounds like someone describing your perfect day.

Sudoku variants are a tremendously satisfying way to flex your mental capabilities. Standard sudoku, of course, is highly popular and highly addictive, with many small "aha!" moments in each puzzle leading to a rush of deductions at the end that leaves you ready for more. But there is a special pleasure in adding additional rules to the mix, giving the opportunity to make entirely new types of deductions.

This book features eight sudoku variants, each with its own chapter, followed by a final chapter which pairs up the variants in different combinations, creating lots of interesting logical interactions. Each chapter begins with an easy puzzle designed to get you accustomed to the way the rules of that variant change the solving process. Of course, even an easier puzzle can start out seeming challenging until you get used to the rules, so check the tips on the first page of each chapter for advice on how to get started. The following puzzles will get more challenging as you go, followed by a final two puzzles that feature an extra twist. Those puzzles won't necessarily be the hardest in the chapter, but they will definitely require a fresh perspective. Difficulty levels are represented on a scale from 1 to 5 stars—but of course difficulty is subjective, so consider those ratings our best estimates.

Happy solving!

EXTRA REGIONS SUDOKU

One of the most straightforward variants of sudoku but a longtime favorite of mine, Extra Regions Sudoku features one or more gray areas containing nine cells each (usually connected horizontally and vertically), which must contain the digits from 1 to 9 once each, just like a standard sudoku region. These regions can take a variety of shapes, even some … unexpected ones, as you will see. This puzzle type is a good introduction to sudoku variants, since the additional constraint is easy to understand—but don't get ahead of yourself! An easy set of rules does not always make an easy puzzle….

In this first chapter you will be presented with eight puzzles that make use of the basic Extra Regions Sudoku rules, ranging from easy to hard, followed by two additional puzzles that will twist these rules in peculiar ways and encourage you to look for new solving techniques—and maybe even force you to forget some old ones. Good luck, and enjoy!

What to look for in an Extra Regions Sudoku

- Focusing on one value at a time can be a good strategy. Puzzle 1 can be solved entirely by first placing all the 1s, then all the 2s, and so on.
- You don't always need to know the exact position of a digit. As long as you have proved that it must belong to a certain set of cells that are all part of the same extra group, it guarantees that this digit may not belong to any other cell in that extra group, which may allow you to make a placement in a different row, column, or region.
- Sometimes, a standard 3×3 region and an extra group will have a lot of cells in common. Use this to your advantage by noticing that the cells of the 3×3 region that don't belong to the extra group will contain the same digits as the cells of the extra group that don't belong to the 3×3 region. For instance, if the two regions share four digits, the five digits they *don't* share must match.

Extra Regions 1
★☆☆☆☆

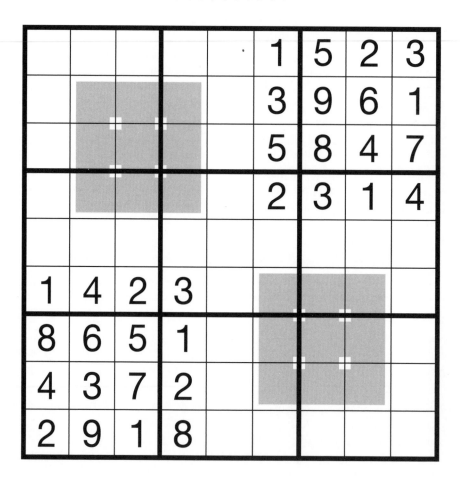

Answer on page 106.

Extra Regions 2

★★☆☆☆

	5	7				4	1	
	6						2	
	9		1	2	3		8	
	7		4	5	6		3	
	2			7			4	
				8				
				1				

Answer on page 106.

Extra Regions 3

★★☆☆☆

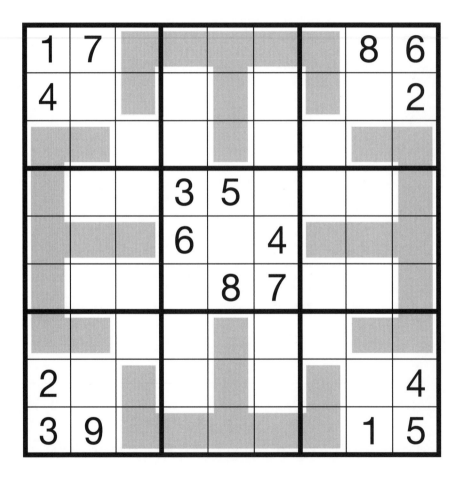

Answer on page 106.

Extra Regions 4
★★★☆☆

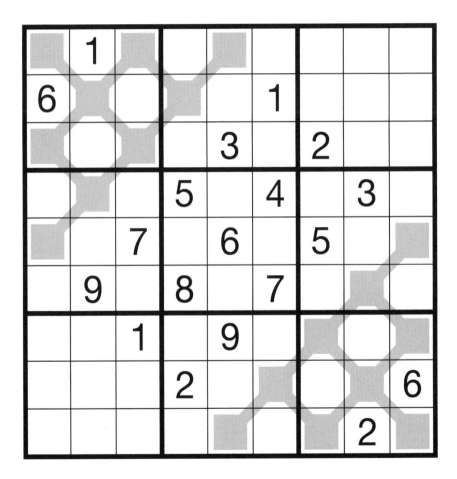

Extra Regions 5
★★★☆☆

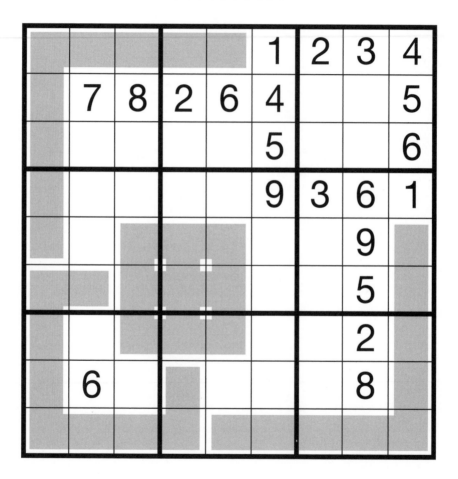

Answer on page 107.

Extra Regions 6
★★★☆☆

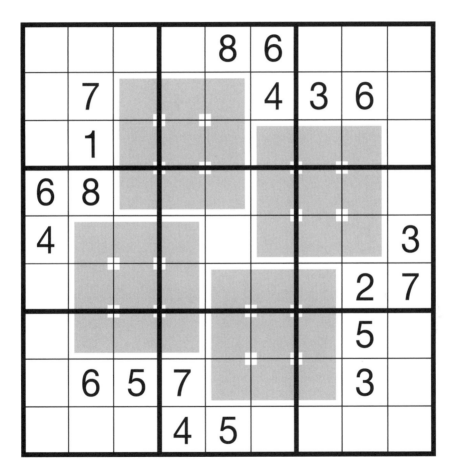

Extra Regions 7
★★★★☆

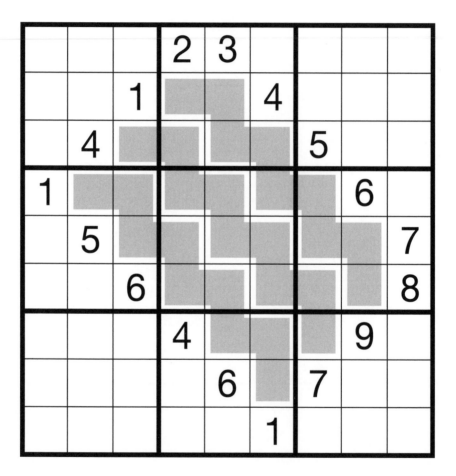

Answer on page 107.

Extra Regions 8
★★★★★

4							9	6
5				1	2			
	8							
	7						3	
							4	
			6	5				3
2	3							8

Liar Region
★★★★☆

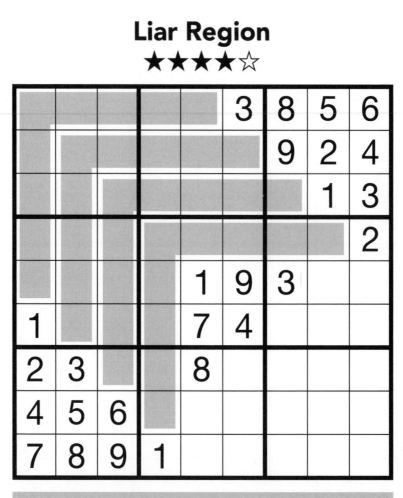

Exactly one of the four given extra regions is a liar and contains at least one repeated digit.

Answer on page 108.

Extra Large Regions
★★★★☆

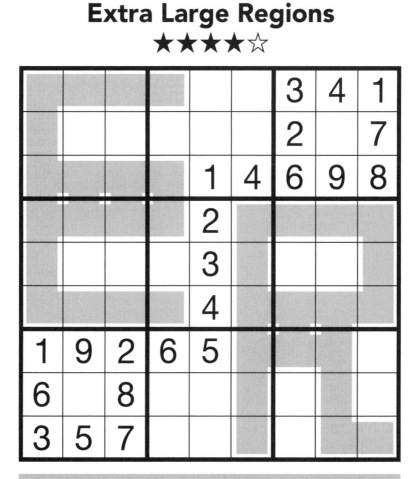

Each 18-cell extra region must contain the digits from 1 to 9 exactly *twice*.

ODD-EVEN SUDOKU

Playing with parity is one of the easiest ways to introduce a slight twist in the rules of sudoku. In this variant, some even digits (2, 4, 6, 8) have been indicated by gray squares, and some odd digits (1, 3, 5, 7, 9) by gray circles. An even digit can never occupy a cell with a circle, nor can an odd digit occupy a cell with a square.

Odd-Even Sudoku is a variant whose potential, I feel, has long been underused. Often in such puzzles, all the symbols for every square in the grid are given, effectively splitting the sudoku into two different puzzles that have no interaction with each other: one using 2, 4, 6 and 8 and the other using 1, 3, 5, 7 and 9. However, this is not what you are going to find here. Instead, you will be given the parity of only some of the cells. This makes it possible to create visually stunning designs, as well as to take advantage of new logical techniques.

What to look for in an Odd-Even Sudoku

- Even digits and odd ones are not equal. In a sudoku there are five odd digits, but only four even ones; this means that you are usually better off focusing on squares than circles, at least at the start. Apply this on puzzle 1: you will find that you can fill all the given shaded squares right from the very beginning.
- At times it can be wise to use symbols for their "blocking" ability rather than for the information they provide about their own cells. Focus on a value and use symbols of the opposite parity to restrict this value's options in a row, column, or region.
- Every bit of knowledge counts in sudoku. Using cells whose parity you already know, try to find the parity of other cells. To do so, keep in mind that rows, columns, and regions must contain exactly four even digits and five odd ones.

Odd-Even 1

★☆☆☆☆

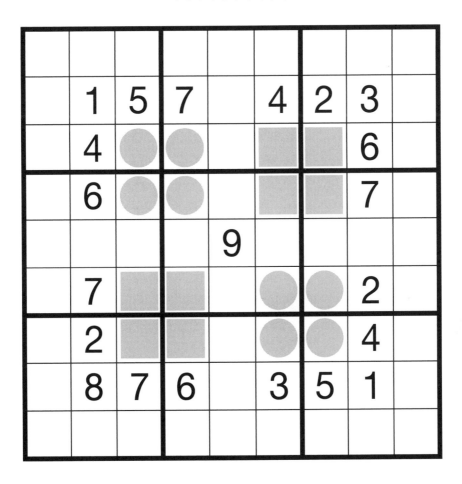

Odd-Even 2
★★☆☆☆

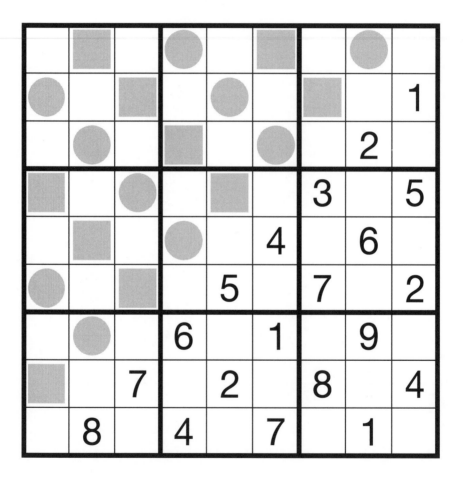

Answer on page 108.

Odd-Even 3

★★☆☆☆

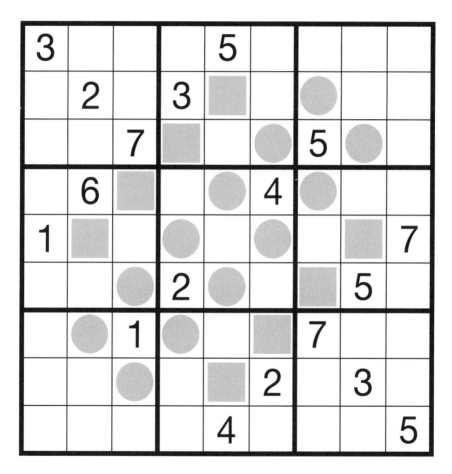

Odd-Even 4
★★★☆☆

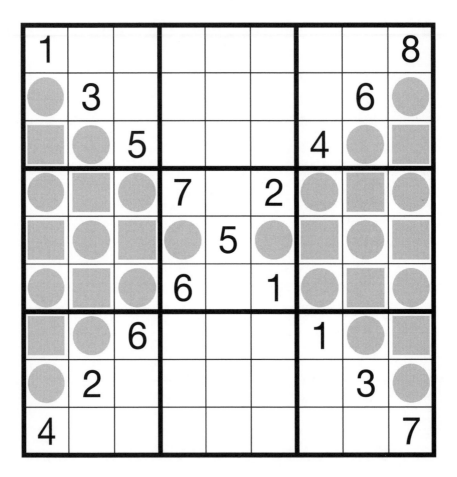

Answer on page 109.

Odd-Even 5

★★★☆☆

		7					⬜	
	2	⚫	3				9	⬜
3	⚫	⚫	⚫	8				
	3	⚫	2					
		6				3		
					7	⬜	2	
				9	⬜	⬜	⬜	4
⚫	8				1	⬜	3	
	⚫				7			

Odd-Even 6
★★★☆☆

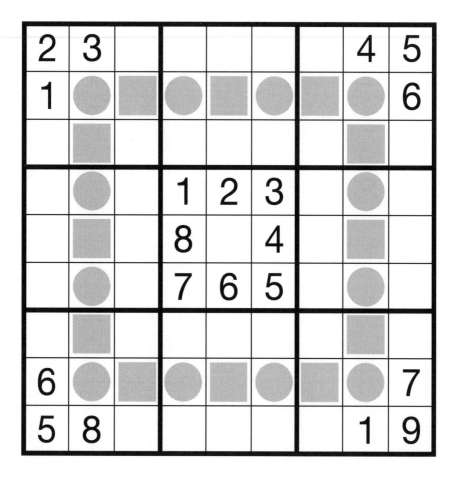

Answer on page 109.

Odd-Even 7
★★★★☆

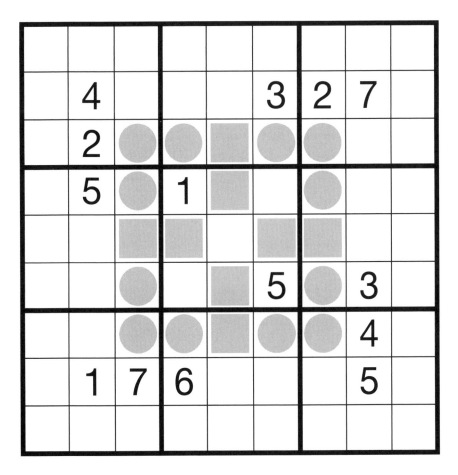

Odd-Even 8
★★★★★

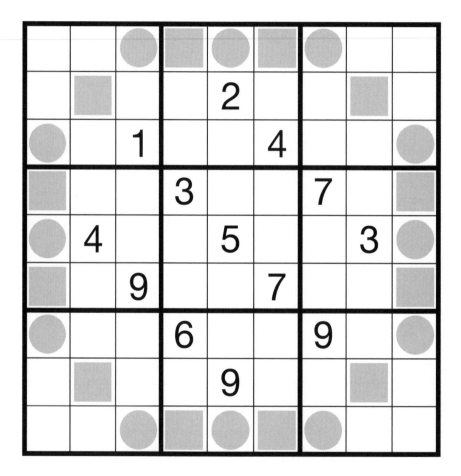

Liar Odd-Even
★★★★☆

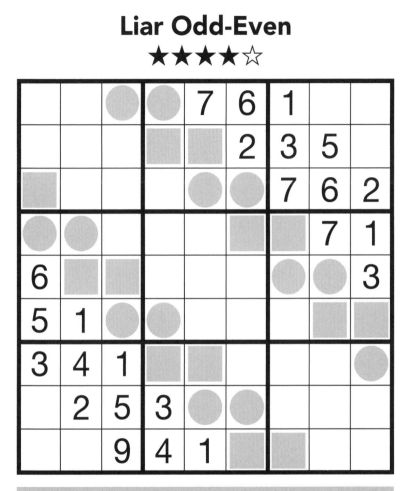

Exactly one of the given symbols is a liar and does not obey the standard Odd-Even rule. It may be either a square containing an odd digit, or a circle containing an even digit.

Mostly Odd-Even
★★★★☆

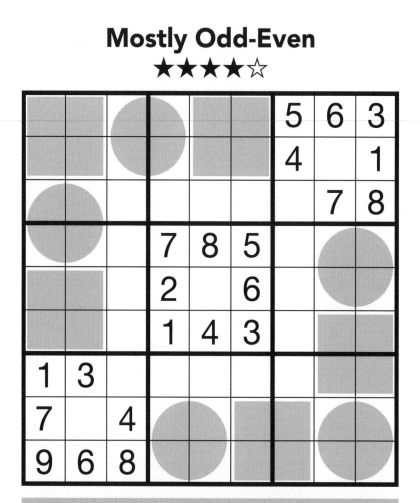

Where four cells are overlapped by a circle, these cells contain more odd digits than even ones. Where four cells are overlapped by a square, these cells contain more even digits than odd ones.

Answer on page 110.

THERMO SUDOKU

Thermo Sudoku was born from a variant that used inequality signs to indicate numerical relationships between adjacent cells; puzzlemakers and solvers alike quickly came to the conclusion that the modification was a clear improvement over the original, and over time it became one of the most popular variants among competitive players. It features a number of thermometers drawn in the grid, all with the following, intuitive property: on a given thermometer, digits must increase as they get further away from the bulb.

This variant can look a bit intimidating for less experienced solvers, as puzzles often include very few given digits. But once you get started, you'll find that the thermometers provide a lot of information. A final note: in some of the harder puzzles, multiple lines may branch off from the same bulb. When this is the case, digits on each line are completely independent from each other after they split (but the digits on each line will increase as they move away from the bulb).

What to look for in a Thermo Sudoku

- The longer the thermometer, the fewer the options: each cell of a length-8 thermometer has only two choices. And although you won't see many of them, when you spot a thermometer of length 9, you can immediately fill all its cells with the digits from 1 to 9 in order. (Puzzle 1 has such a thermometer, as it happens.)
- Focusing on extreme values is always a good idea. 1s can only appear on the bulb of a thermometer; 9s, only at the tip. Other values are less restricted, of course, but 2s and 8s are also well worth your attention.
- A smart use of pencil marks is recommended. Thermometers can often interact with each other, and you will have an easier time spotting it if you focus your attention on cells with only two or three options, which can reveal a useful pair or triple.

Thermo 1
★☆☆☆☆

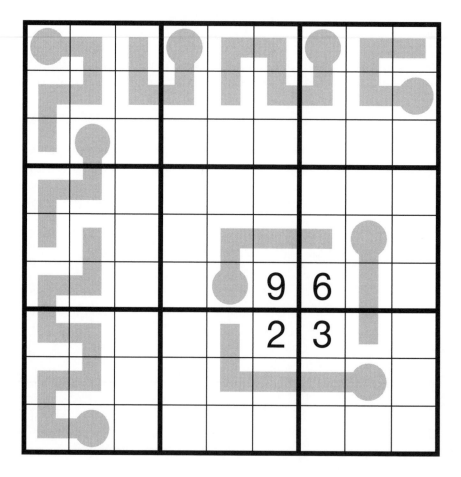

Answer on page 111.

Thermo 2

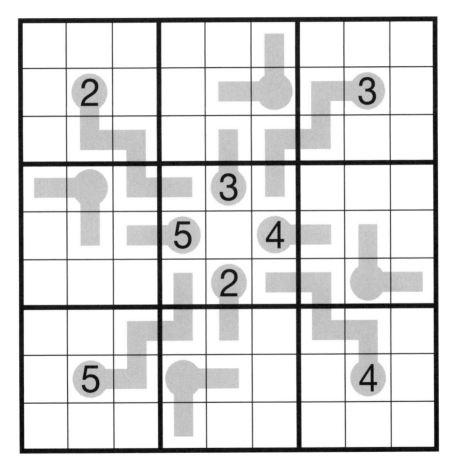

Thermo 3
★★☆☆☆

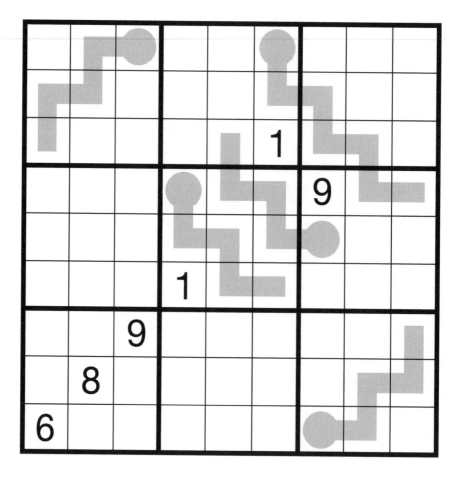

Answer on page 111.

Thermo 4
★★★☆☆

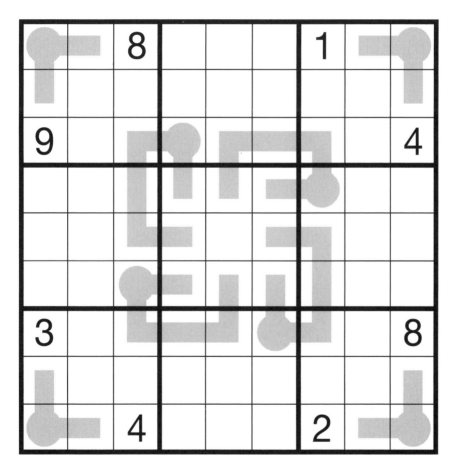

Thermo 5
★★★☆☆

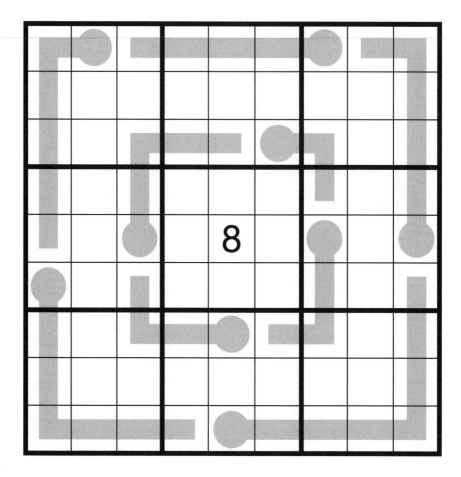

Answer on page 112.

Thermo 6

★★★☆☆

					1			
			2		3			

Answer on page 112.

Thermo 7
★★★★☆

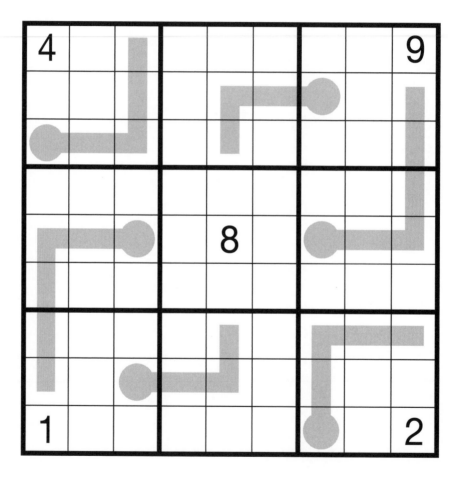

Answer on page 112.

Thermo 8

★★★★★

			1	2	3			
			8		4			
			7	6	5			

Invisibulbs
★★★☆☆

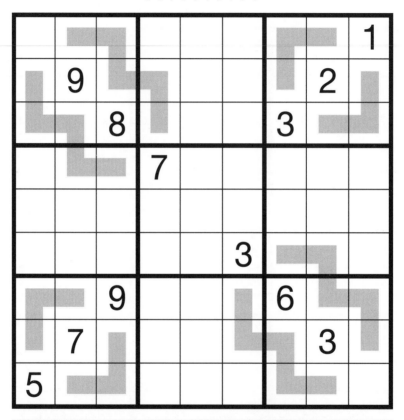

The bulb of each thermometer is invisible, but it is always located at an end of the line. There is exactly one bulb on each thermometer.

Answer on page 113.

Broken Thermometer
★★★☆☆

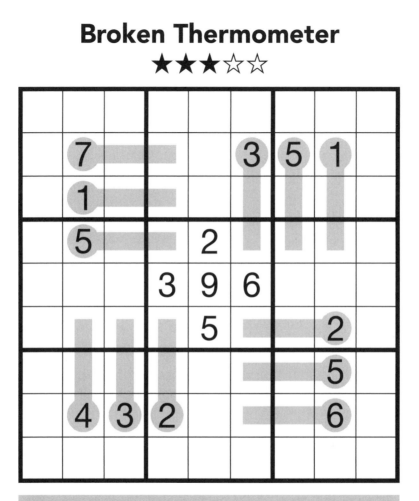

Exactly one of the given thermometers is a liar and does not obey the standard Thermo rule. (One or more digits within that thermometer may contradict the rule.)

KILLER SUDOKU

In Killer Sudoku, dotted cages are drawn in the grid, each having its own clue in the upper left corner. No digit can be repeated within a dotted cage, and clues give the sum of all digits in their respective cages.

For me, this is another puzzle type that never gets old. However, Killer Sudoku is as dreaded by some as it is loved by others—such is the fate of any variant that introduces an arithmetical element to sudoku. As a sudoku variant, though, it offers a lot of depth. These puzzles do not give up without a fight, but they are also particularly rewarding to solve!

What to look for in a Killer Sudoku

- For most cage sizes, there are exactly four possible clue values that can each be obtained from only one combination of digits: the two biggest ones and the two smallest ones. For example, for a cage of size 3, these are 6 (1 + 2 + 3), 7 (1 + 2 + 4), 23 (6 + 8 + 9), and 24 (7 + 8 + 9). You may be familiar with this technique if you've solved kakuro, also known as cross sums. These values are extremely useful for getting started on a puzzle, as they will provide you with pairs and triples that will strongly restrict the options of other cages. This is exactly how you should start puzzle 1, by looking at the size-3 cages in the top two corners and seeing how they affect nearby size-2 cages.
- The sum of all the digits from 1 to 9 is 45, meaning that each row, column, and region contains digits that add up to 45. This can be used in conjunction with dotted cages to determine the value of some cells; one of the most common ways to do this is by summing cages that are all included in a region, and thereby finding the total value of the cells that belong to that region but are not part of a cage. Of course, this can be extended to more than just one row, column, or region.

Killer 1

★☆☆☆☆

Killer 2

★★☆☆☆

Answer on page 113.

Killer 3

Killer 4

★★★☆☆

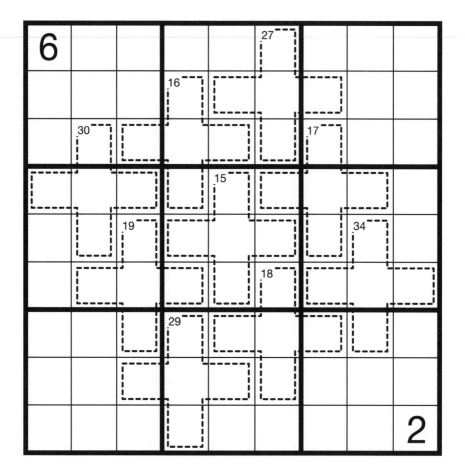

Answer on page 114.

Killer 5

★★★★☆

Killer 6

★★★★☆

20		20			20		20	
	15					16		
20			2	7	1		20	
	4					7		
	6					9		
20	9					5	20	
	18		4	3	8	17		
20		20			20		20	

Answer on page 114.

Killer 7

★★★★☆

Killer 8

★★★★★

Answer on page 115.

Killer Sums

★★☆☆☆

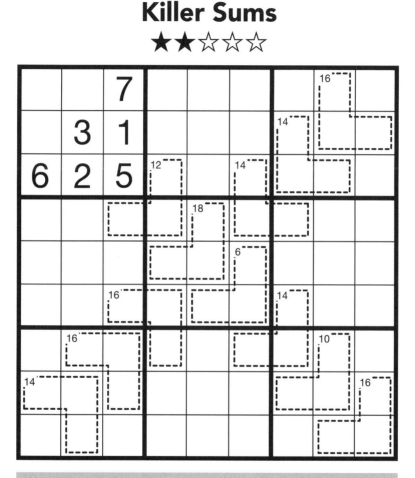

On top of the standard Killer rules, the following additional rule applies: in each dotted cage, one of the digits is equal to the sum of the other two.

Liar Killer

★★★★☆

9		9		9			11	8
10		10		10				
		9			6	11	8
11	13		4	2			
			7			11	8
11	13		9	8			
	5			2		
11	13	10	12	14	
		9	9	9	

Exactly one of the dotted cages is a liar and does not obey the standard Killer rule, meaning its digits do not add up to the total given in the upper left.

Answer on page 115.

CLONE SUDOKU

One or more shapes cloned one or more times—that's the basic idea behind Clone Sudoku, and it's as straightforward as it gets. Each grid will contain one or more sets of identical gray shapes (also the same size and orientation), and within each set, each shape must contain the same set of digits in the same locations. That's all there is to it, but that's enough to design some devious puzzles.

One important detail to note is that, unlike Extra Region Sudoku, digits are freely allowed to repeat within a gray shape as long as the placement does not contradict the rules of classic sudoku, so be careful not to draw hasty conclusions.

What to look for in a Clone Sudoku

- In easier puzzles, it will often be enough to focus on individual cloned cells, one group at a time. If you find a group of cloned cells that, between them, "see" many given digits (that is, share a row, column, or region with them), you should be able to narrow down the options for those cells—possibly all the way down to just one. Proceed this way to solve puzzle 1, by first focusing on the 2×2 squares, one cell at a time.
- In intermediate puzzles where gray cells cannot be solved right away, focusing on one value at a time can prove to be helpful. Use gray cells to limit the options for that digit in a particular row, column, or region, much like you did with Odd-Even Sudoku.
- Some harder puzzles will need you to look for additional "cloned cells" outside of given gray shapes. That is, you may find a cell for which you will not be able to determine its value, but still be able to locate some other cells that must share the same value. Assign the same letter, or color, to a set of such cells and see what options are left for this letter/color in other rows, columns, or regions. With a bit of back-and-forth, you may well be able to find its value eventually.

Clone 1

★☆☆☆☆

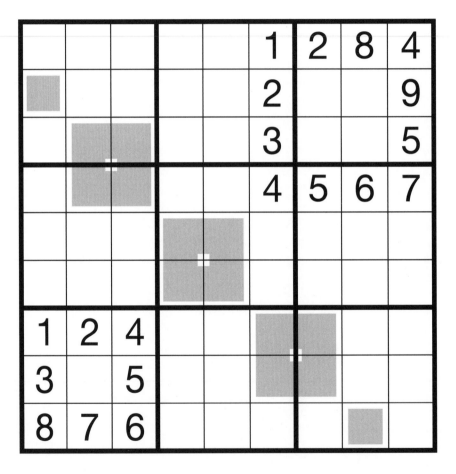

Answer on page 116.

Clone 2

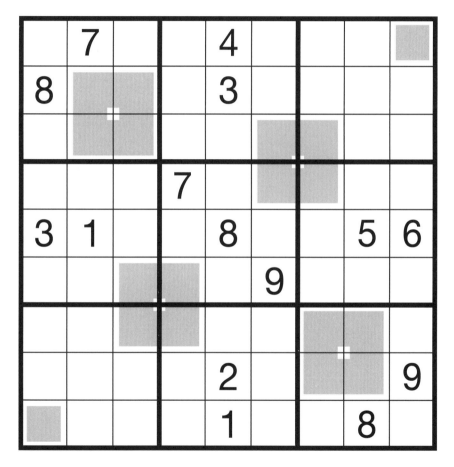

Clone 3

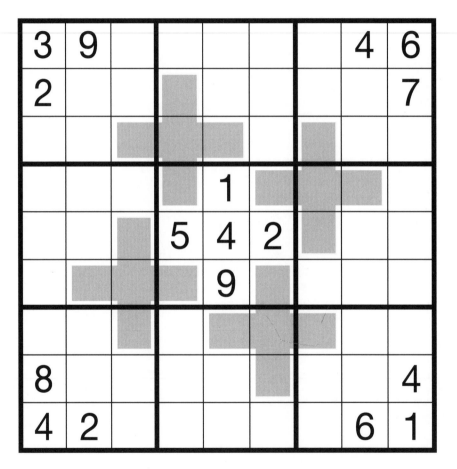

Answer on page 116.

Clone 4

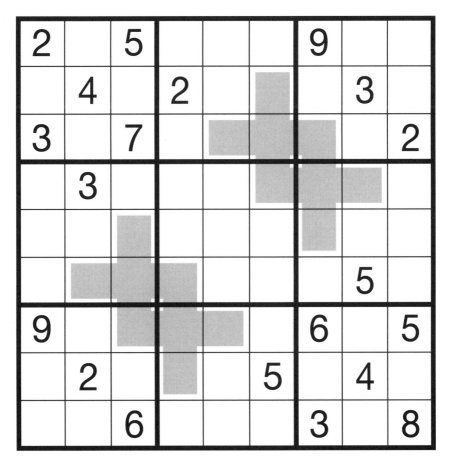

Clone 5

★★★☆☆

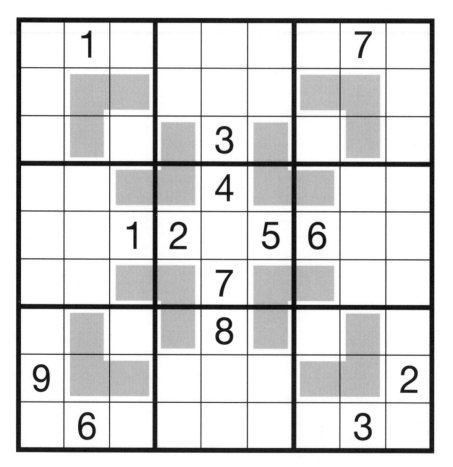

Clone 6

★★★☆☆

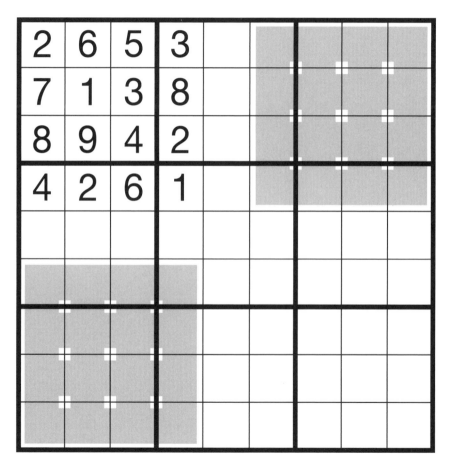

Clone 7

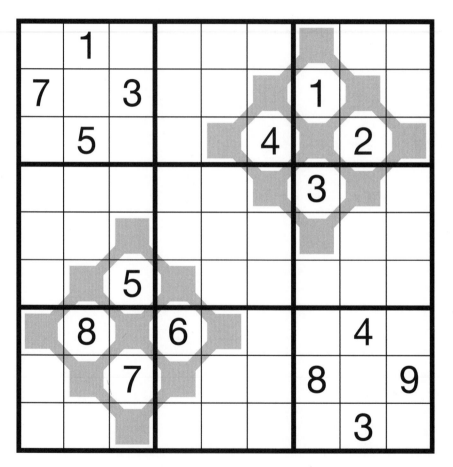

Clone 8
★★★★★

	2	3				8	1	
	1	4				7	9	
					6	3		
	7	9			5	4		
	4	1						

Invisible Clone
★★★☆☆

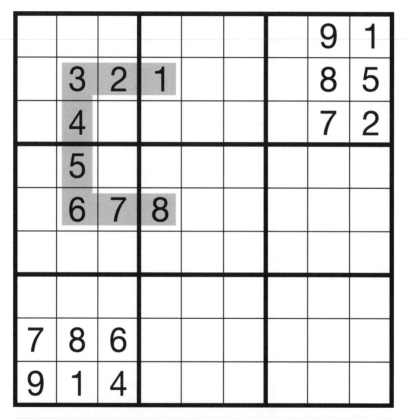

The given gray shape has exactly one clone, which is hidden somewhere in the grid. The clone has not been rotated nor reflected.

Answer on page 118.

Liar Clone

★★★★☆

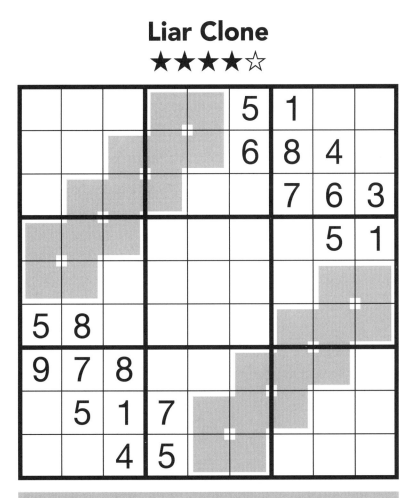

The two gray shapes are regular clones, except for exactly one pair of corresponding cells that do not contain the same digit.

Answer on page 118.

CONSECUTIVE PAIRS SUDOKU

Consecutive Pairs Sudoku revolves around a simple idea: a dot between a pair of cells means that the digits in those two cells must be consecutive (that is, they differ by 1). There is a related variant that you may be familiar with, commonly called Consecutive Sudoku, in which *every* adjacent pair of consecutive digits in the grid is marked. But in Consecutive Pairs Sudoku, not all the pairs are necessarily marked, meaning that the lack of a dot between two cells tells you nothing about their relationship.

As a puzzlemaker as well as a solver, I must confess an inclination towards this variant rather than its counterpart, as it allows more control over the solving path and, as a consequence, the difficulty—as well as enabling the construction of puzzles with a stunning look.

What to look for in a Consecutive Pairs Sudoku

- The longer the chain formed by a series of consecutive cells, the fewer the options. Just be careful to note that digits may repeat along such a chain (unless, of course, they share a row, column, or region).
- Each digit is consecutive to exactly two others—except for 1 and 9, which are each consecutive to only a single digit. Any given digit that touches a dot, then, will give you a lot of information, possibly giving you another digit immediately, and at worst restricting one cell to only two options.
- Consecutive digits must be of different parities. This means that along a chain of dot-linked cells, even and odd digits will alternate. This observation can prove very helpful in order to limit the options for some cells, and will make your job easier in some of the harder puzzles.

Consecutive Pairs 1

★☆☆☆☆

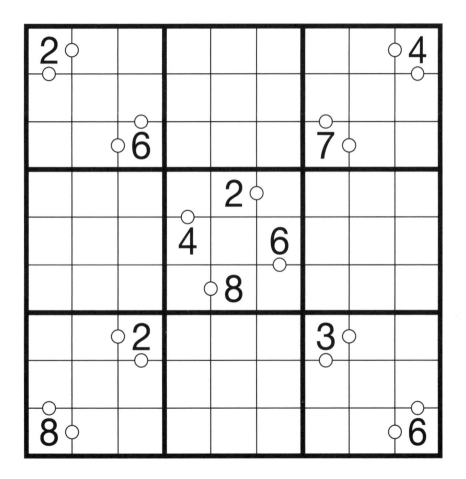

Consecutive Pairs 2

★★☆☆☆

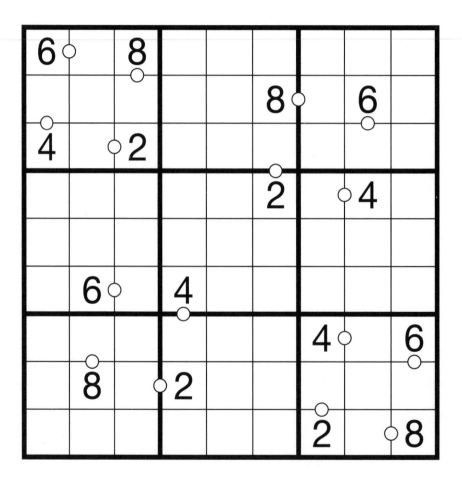

Answer on page 118.

Consecutive Pairs 3
★★☆☆☆

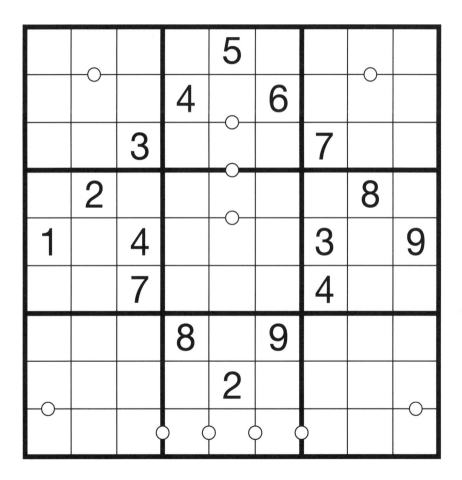

Consecutive Pairs 4

★★☆☆☆

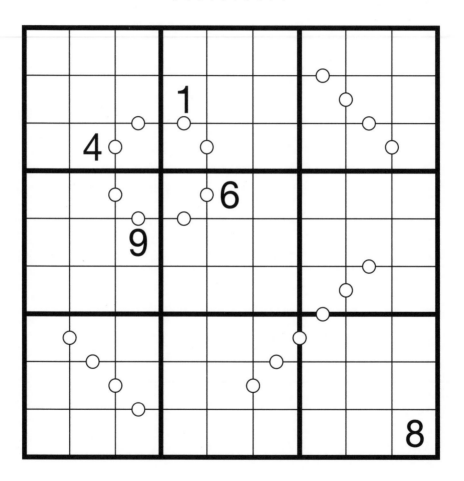

Answer on page 119.

Consecutive Pairs 5

★★★☆☆

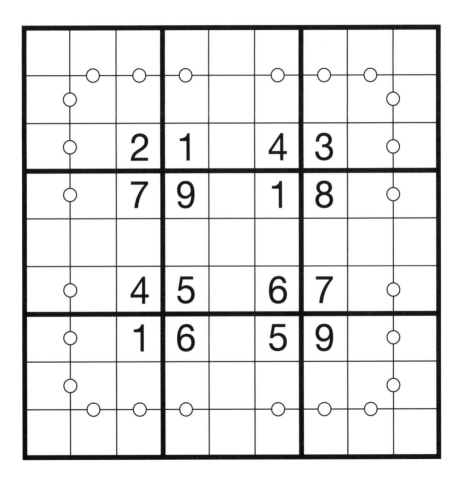

Consecutive Pairs 6

★★★☆☆

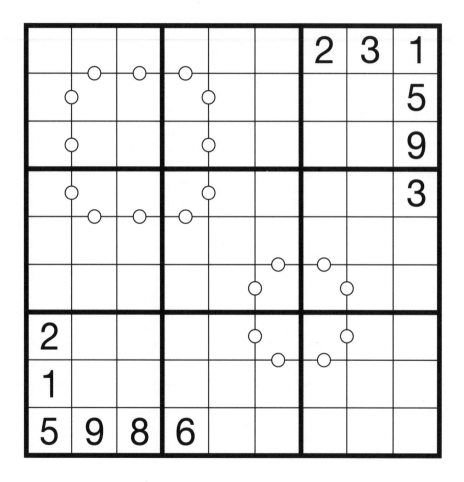

Consecutive Pairs 7

★★★★☆

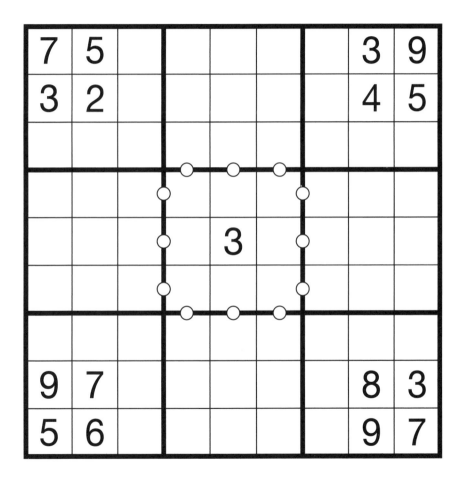

Consecutive Pairs 8
★★★★☆

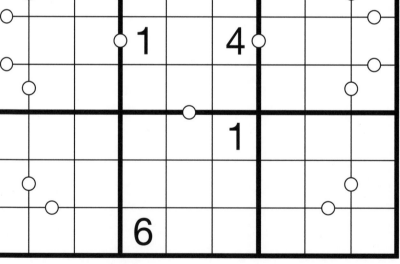

Answer on page 120.

Greater Than Consecutive Pairs

★★★☆☆

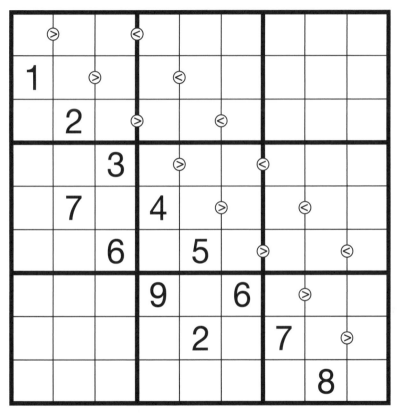

The standard rules for Consecutive Pairs Sudoku apply. Additionally, digits must obey the inequality symbols (the larger digit must be on the side of the open end of the symbol; e.g., 2>1, 8<9).

Answer on page 120.

Nonconsecutive Pairs
★★★☆☆

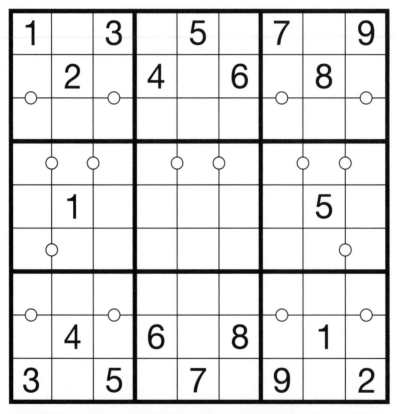

Two cells that are separated by a white dot may *not* contain consecutive digits (that is, they must differ by at least 2).

Answer on page 120.

ZONES SUDOKU

Zones Sudoku is a type I came up with many years ago, as a way to introduce beginner solvers to variants of sudoku. It has since then gained a bit of popularity in the competitive world, where it occasionally surfaces. Its rules are the definition of simplicity: dotted cages are drawn in the grid; some digits are given as a clue in the upper left of each cage, meaning that these digits must appear somewhere in the corresponding cage.

Out of this simplest of ideas, one can make a number of interesting and challenging puzzles by playing with the size and shape of cages, and by being more or less generous with the numbered clues.

What to look for in a Zones Sudoku

- When a cage of size N has exactly N digits given as its clue, it means that you already know its contents. In particular, a size-2 cage with a two-digit clue is effectively a pair, which you can use as if you were solving a classic sudoku. Understanding this concept and focusing on how the different cages' pairs interact is all you'll need to solve puzzle 1.
- A clue that contains one or more repeated digits is often a great starting point, as these digits will be forced to occupy as many rows/columns/regions as there are occurrences of them.
- In harder puzzles, you may need to focus more on cells that are *outside* of cages rather than on filling the cages themselves.

Zones 1

★☆☆☆☆

Answer on page 121.

Zones 2

★★☆☆☆

Zones 3

★★☆☆☆

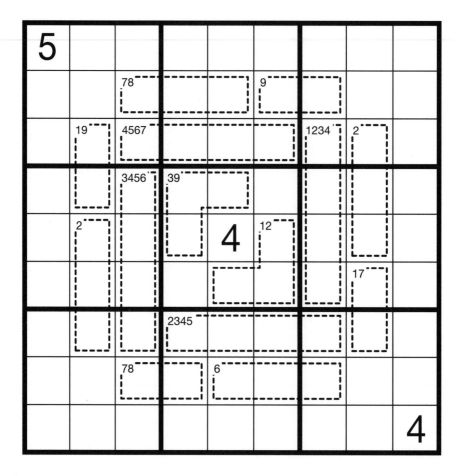

Answer on page 121.

Zones 4
★★★☆☆

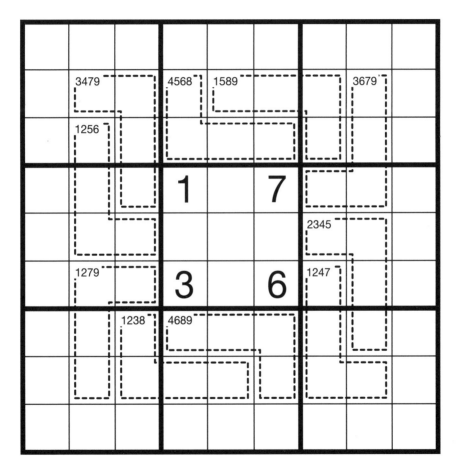

Zones 5

★★★☆☆

Answer on page 122.

Zones 6

★★★★☆

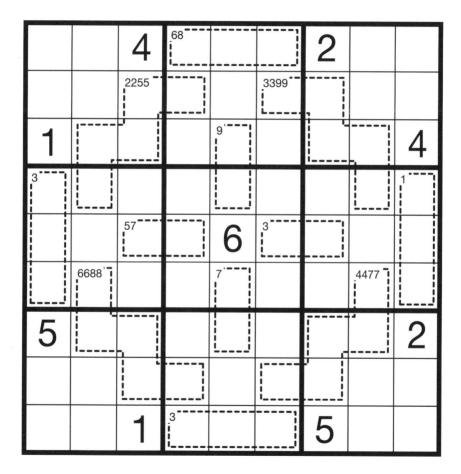

Zones 7

★★★★☆

1		2		3		4		5
8	9		1		2		3	
	6	2		7		9		6
7		5	4		5		8	
	8		9			5		7
6		4		1			6	
	7		3		4			8
5		6		9		2		
	3		2		1		9	

Zones 8
★★★★★

	335577	8			
224466					446688
	5	147	368	**2**	
1					2
		5			
	249		167		
	1			**5**	
	557799				
		246			

Liar Zones

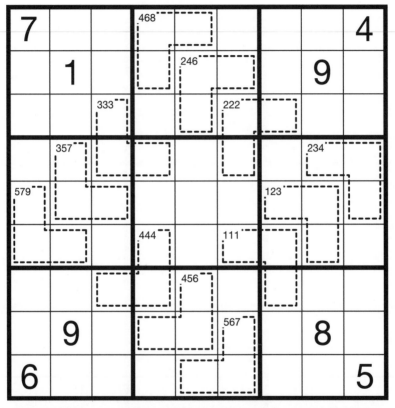

Each dotted cage must contain exactly *two* of the three digits given as its clue.

Answer on page 123.

Pick One Zone

★★★☆☆

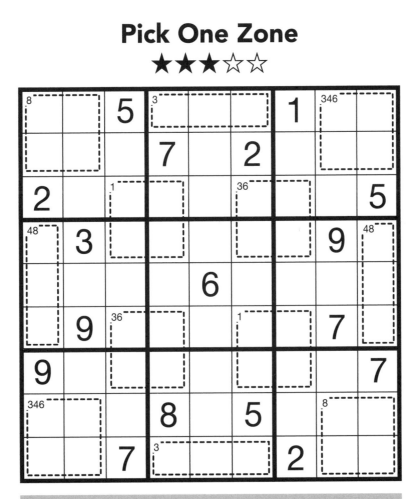

Each dotted cage has an identically shaped, symmetrically located twin that has the same clue. For each such pair of cages, one must contain the digit or digits given as its clue; the other one may *not* contain any of these digits.

RENBAN GROUPS SUDOKU

This variant, of Japanese origin, is one of my all-time favorites. A renban group is a set of unique digits that can be ordered to form a consecutive series (for example, 2-3-4-5-6). Each gray shape must contain such a group; the digits may be placed in any order within the gray shape.

You should know the drill by now. Eight standard Renban Groups Sudoku puzzles are waiting for you, followed by two twisty puzzles that add, take out, or alter a little something. Will you be up to the task?

What to look for in a Renban Groups Sudoku

- Extreme values are your friends. If a group contains a 1 or a 9, you can tell instantly what the remaining digits must be. Apply this idea to puzzle 1 and you should see the end of it in no time.
- The larger the group, the smaller the number of possibilities: the sheer size of a shape is a very useful clue in itself, even if said shape is empty. A renban group of size 5 will always contain a 5. A group of size 6 has to contain a 4, a 5, and a 6 … and so on.
- A group of size N can only contain digits whose difference is at most N–1. This comes into play in conjunction with extreme values; for instance, if you can prove that a group of size 6 must contain an 8, then 1 and 2 will be eliminated as possibilities within that group (since 3-4-5-6-7-8 and 4-5-6-7-8-9 are the only options). It will often prove more useful to focus on these excluded values than on the digits that have to belong to the group.
- A more tricky use of this principle is to restrict potential values in some cells. If a size-6 group contains a cell that has 1 and 8 as its only options, then no other cells in the group can contain either of these two digits, since that would force both 1 and 8 to belong to the same size-6 group—which is, of course, impossible.

Renban Groups 1

★☆☆☆☆

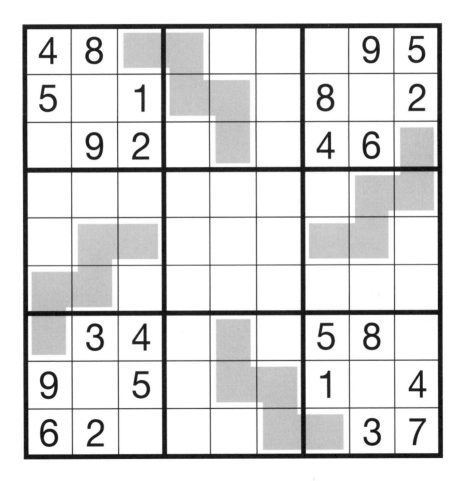

Renban Groups 2
★★☆☆☆

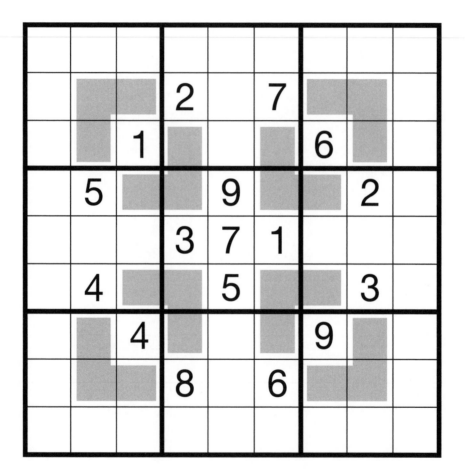

Answer on page 123.

Renban Groups 3

★★☆☆☆

					7			
					4	5		
	5				6			
5	8	4						
						1	8	2
			6				7	
		6	5					
			8					

Renban Groups 4
★★★☆☆

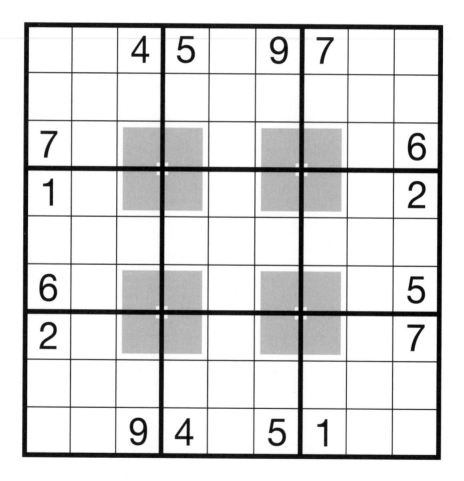

Answer on page 124.

Renban Groups 5

★★★☆☆

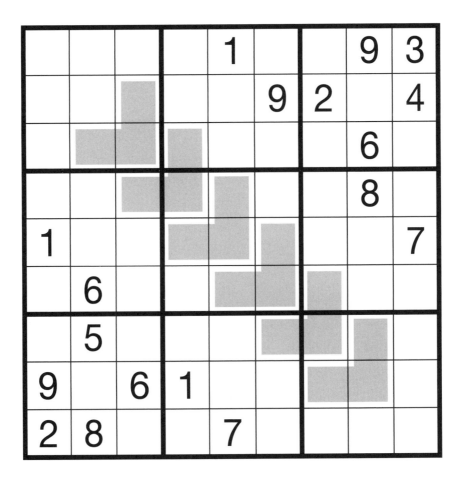

Renban Groups 6
★★★☆☆

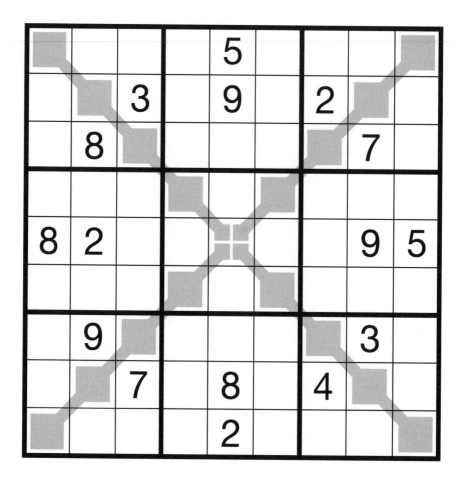

Answer on page 124.

Renban Groups 7

★★★★☆

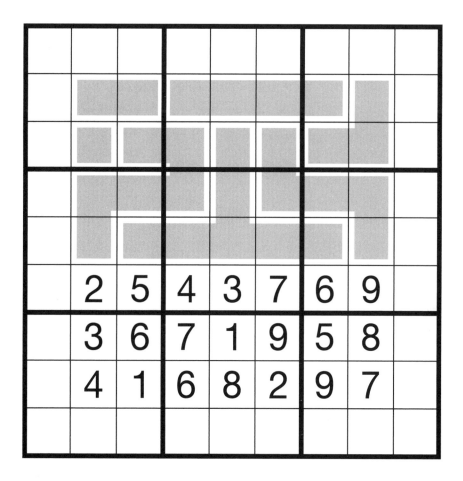

Renban Groups 8
★★★★★

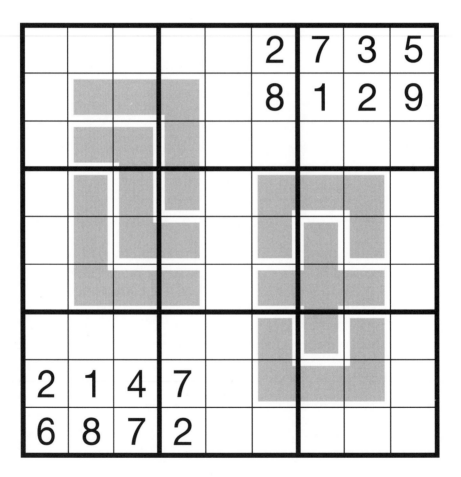

Answer on page 125.

Anti-Renban Groups

★★★☆☆

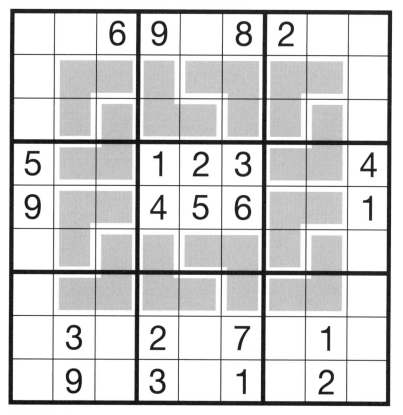

Gray shapes may not contain *any* consecutive digits, regardless of their positions. All digits within a gray shape must be different.

Unique Renban Groups

★★★★☆

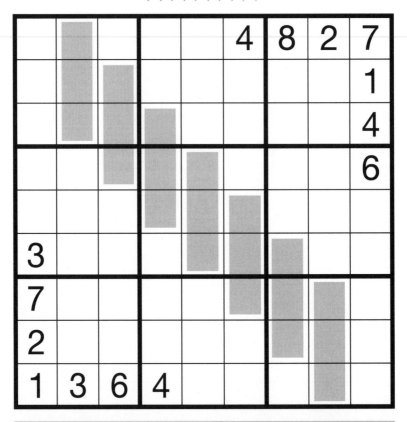

The standard rules for Renban Groups Sudoku apply. Additionally, no two groups may contain the same set of digits (in any order).

Answer on page 125.

HYBRIDS

Here comes the final treat: a set of twelve hybrid puzzles, each (with one exception) combining two different rules in a more or less tricky way. While most, such as the puzzle titled "Clone/Zones," have got nothing to hide and use both rules of the relevant variants in the simplest manner, some, like the mysterious "Extra Regions or Clones?" will introduce you to a second layer of complexity: there, your first task will be to find out where you should apply each constraint, as extra groups and cloned shapes will be indistinguishable.

The puzzles in this chapter cover a broad range of difficulties and are roughly ordered from the easiest to the hardest, but be aware that your feelings may differ greatly based on which variants you have the most affinity for, so—take the ratings with a pinch of salt. And if you've skipped ahead to this chapter and find yourself struggling with a particular puzzle, you may want to revisit the earlier chapters to hone your skills....

What to look for in Hybrids

- No tips, no tricks: this time, you are on your own. Apply what you learned in the previous chapters, but pay particular attention to the way the pairs of variants interact with each other; there lies the key to success. Good luck with tackling this last set of challenges!

Extra Regions or Clones?

★★☆☆☆

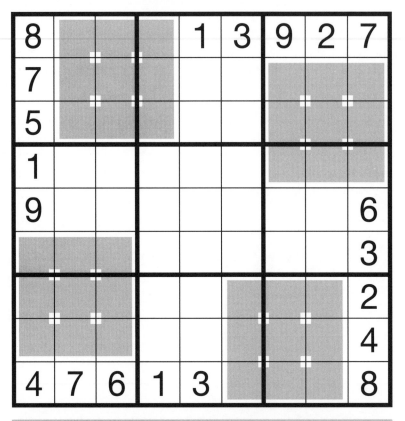

Two of the four given shapes are regular extra regions; the two others are clones. It is up to you to determine which is which.

Answer on page 126.

Renban Groups/Extra Regions

★★☆☆☆

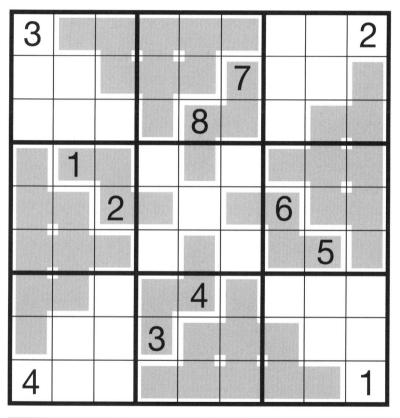

The standard rules for Renban Groups Sudoku and Extra Regions Sudoku apply.

Extra Regions/Odd-Even
★★★☆☆

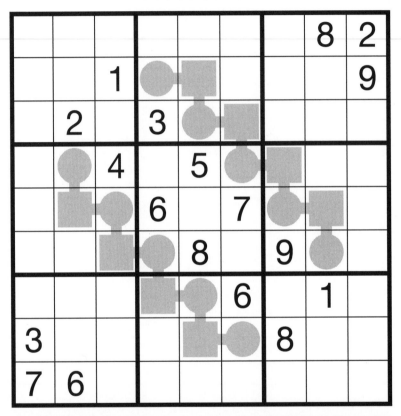

The standard rules of Odd-Even Sudoku apply. Additionally, the given symbols form two sets of nine cells, linked orthogonally. These two sets behave like regular extra regions, meaning no digit can be repeated in either set.

Answer on page 126.

Consecutive Pairs/Renban Groups

★★★☆☆

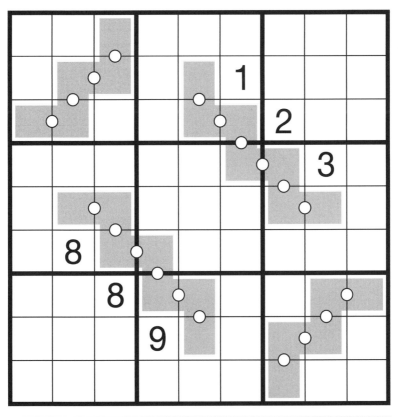

The standard rules for Consecutive Pairs Sudoku and Renban Groups Sudoku apply.

Thermo Killer
★★★☆☆

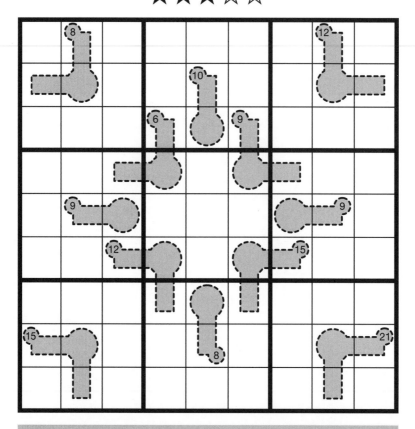

Each thermometer shape behaves like a regular thermometer as well as a standard killer cage (digits cannot be repeated within a cage, and they must sum to the total given).

Answer on page 127.

Clone/Zones

★★★☆☆

The standard rules for Clone Sudoku and Zones Sudoku apply.

Renban Groups/Killer

★★★★☆

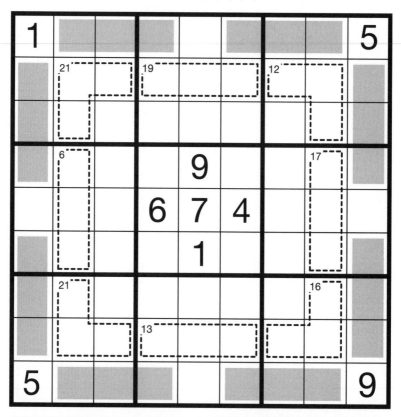

The standard rules for Renban Groups Sudoku and Killer Sudoku apply.

Answer on page 127.

Consecutive Pairs/Odd-Even
★★★★☆

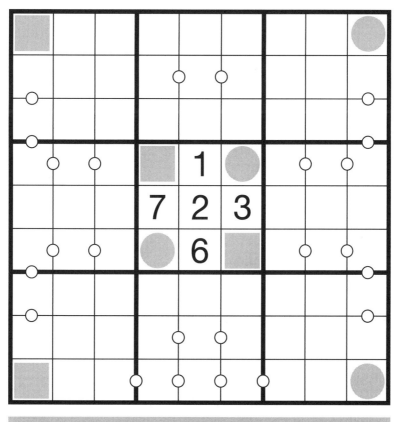

The standard rules for Consecutive Pairs Sudoku and Odd-Even Sudoku apply.

Answer on page 127.

Zones or Killer?

★★★★☆

Each dotted cage is either a Killer Sudoku cage or a Zones Sudoku cage. It is up to you to determine which rule applies to which cage. (Note that the digits in a Zones clue may appear in any order.)

Answer on page 128.

Odd-Even/Killer
★★★★☆

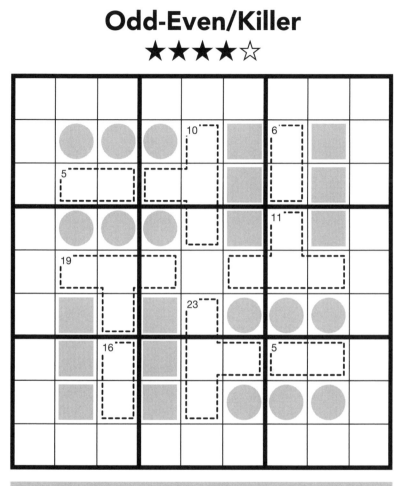

The standard rules for Odd-Even Sudoku and Killer Sudoku apply.

Cloned Thermometers
★★★★★

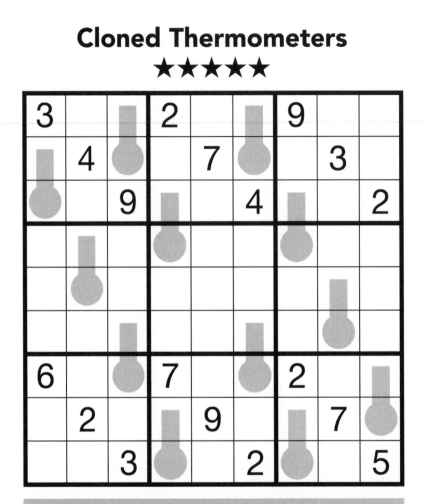

The standard rules for Thermo Sudoku apply. Additionally, each thermometer has exactly two clones hidden among the other thermometers (so there are four groups that each contain three identical thermometers).

Answer on page 128.

All in One
★★★★★

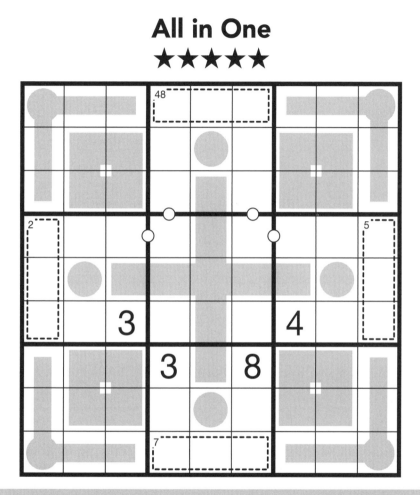

Each of the eight regular rules seen in previous chapters (Extra Regions, Odd-Even, Thermo, Killer, Clone, Consecutive Pairs, Zones, and Renban Groups) is used at least once in this puzzle. In some cases it is up to you to determine which rule applies where. Good luck!

Extra Regions 1

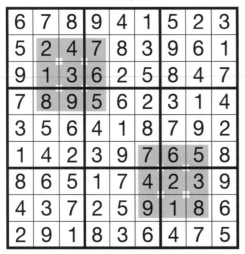

6	7	8	9	4	1	5	2	3
5	2	4	7	8	3	9	6	1
9	1	3	6	2	5	8	4	7
7	8	9	5	6	2	3	1	4
3	5	6	4	1	8	7	9	2
1	4	2	3	9	7	6	5	8
8	6	5	1	7	4	2	3	9
4	3	7	2	5	9	1	8	6
2	9	1	8	3	6	4	7	5

Extra Regions 2

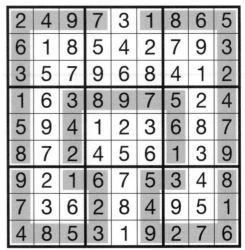

2	4	9	7	3	1	8	6	5
6	1	8	5	4	2	7	9	3
3	5	7	9	6	8	4	1	2
1	6	3	8	9	7	5	2	4
5	9	4	1	2	3	6	8	7
8	7	2	4	5	6	1	3	9
9	2	1	6	7	5	3	4	8
7	3	6	2	8	4	9	5	1
4	8	5	3	1	9	2	7	6

Extra Regions 3

1	7	9	4	2	5	3	8	6
4	6	8	9	7	3	1	5	2
5	2	3	1	6	8	7	4	9
6	8	2	3	5	1	4	9	7
7	3	1	6	9	4	5	2	8
9	5	4	2	8	7	6	3	1
8	4	7	5	1	9	2	6	3
2	1	5	8	3	6	9	7	4
3	9	6	7	4	2	8	1	5

Extra Regions 4

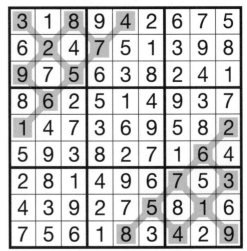

3	1	8	9	4	2	6	7	5
6	2	4	7	5	1	3	9	8
9	7	5	6	3	8	2	4	1
8	6	2	5	1	4	9	3	7
1	4	7	3	6	9	5	8	2
5	9	3	8	2	7	1	6	4
2	8	1	4	9	6	7	5	3
4	3	9	2	7	5	8	1	6
7	5	6	1	8	3	4	2	9

Extra Regions 5

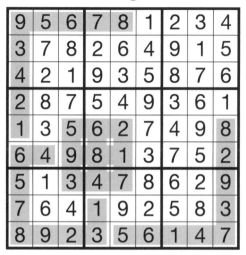

9	5	6	7	8	1	2	3	4
3	7	8	2	6	4	9	1	5
4	2	1	9	3	5	8	7	6
2	8	7	5	4	9	3	6	1
1	3	5	6	2	7	4	9	8
6	4	9	8	1	3	7	5	2
5	1	3	4	7	8	6	2	9
7	6	4	1	9	2	5	8	3
8	9	2	3	5	6	1	4	7

Extra Regions 6

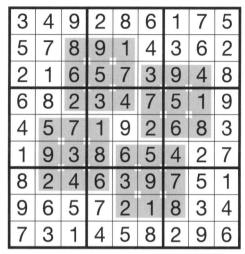

3	4	9	2	8	6	1	7	5
5	7	8	9	1	4	3	6	2
2	1	6	5	7	3	9	4	8
6	8	2	3	4	7	5	1	9
4	5	7	1	9	2	6	8	3
1	9	3	8	6	5	4	2	7
8	2	4	6	3	9	7	5	1
9	6	5	7	2	1	8	3	4
7	3	1	4	5	8	2	9	6

Extra Regions 7

5	7	8	2	3	9	4	1	6
2	6	1	5	7	4	8	3	9
3	4	9	1	8	6	5	7	2
1	8	4	7	2	3	9	6	5
9	5	3	6	4	8	1	2	7
7	2	6	9	1	5	3	4	8
8	1	2	4	5	7	6	9	3
4	9	5	3	6	2	7	8	1
6	3	7	8	9	1	2	5	4

Extra Regions 8

4	2	8	7	3	5	1	9	6
5	9	6	8	1	2	3	7	4
7	1	3	9	6	4	5	8	2
3	8	9	5	4	7	6	2	1
1	7	4	2	9	6	8	3	5
6	5	2	3	8	1	9	4	7
8	6	1	4	2	3	7	5	9
9	4	7	6	5	8	2	1	3
2	3	5	1	7	9	4	6	8

Liar Region

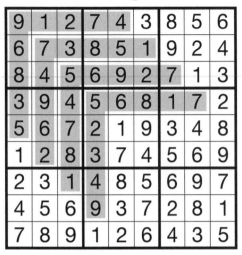

Extra Large Regions

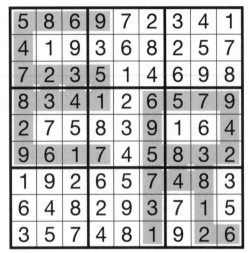

Odd-Even 1

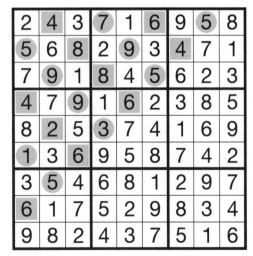

Odd-Even 2

Odd-Even 3

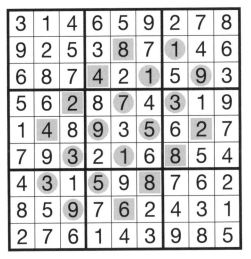

Odd-Even 4

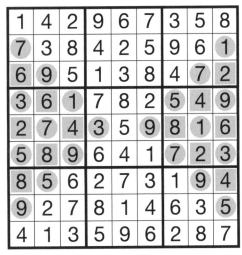

Odd-Even 5

4	6	7	9	2	5	1	8	3
8	2	1	3	7	4	5	9	6
3	5	9	1	8	6	4	7	2
1	3	5	2	6	8	9	4	7
2	7	6	4	1	9	3	5	8
9	4	8	5	3	7	6	2	1
5	1	3	7	9	2	8	6	4
7	8	4	6	5	1	2	3	9
6	9	2	8	4	3	7	1	5

Odd-Even 6

2	3	7	6	1	8	9	4	5
1	5	8	3	4	9	2	7	6
4	6	9	2	5	7	1	8	3
9	7	6	1	2	3	8	5	4
3	2	5	8	9	4	7	6	1
8	1	4	7	6	5	3	9	2
7	4	1	9	3	6	5	2	8
6	9	2	5	8	1	4	3	7
5	8	3	4	7	2	6	1	9

Odd-Even 7

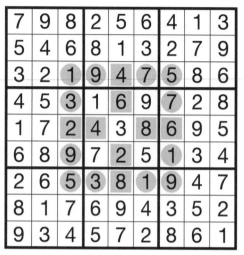

7	9	8	2	5	6	4	1	3
5	4	6	8	1	3	2	7	9
3	2	1	9	4	7	5	8	6
4	5	3	1	6	9	7	2	8
1	7	2	4	3	8	6	9	5
6	8	9	7	2	5	1	3	4
2	6	5	3	8	1	9	4	7
8	1	7	6	9	4	3	5	2
9	3	4	5	7	2	8	6	1

Odd-Even 8

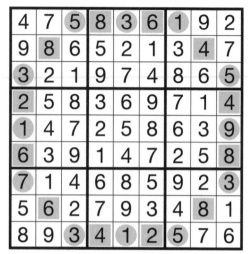

4	7	5	8	3	6	1	9	2
9	8	6	5	2	1	3	4	7
3	2	1	9	7	4	8	6	5
2	5	8	3	6	9	7	1	4
1	4	7	2	5	8	6	3	9
6	3	9	1	4	7	2	5	8
7	1	4	6	8	5	9	2	3
5	6	2	7	9	3	4	8	1
8	9	3	4	1	2	5	7	6

Liar Odd-Even

2	5	3	9	7	6	1	4	8
1	7	6	8	4	2	3	5	9
4	9	8	1	5	3	7	6	2
9	3	2	5	8	4	6	7	1
6	8	4	7	2	1	5	9	3
5	1	7	6	3	9	8	2	4
3	4	1	2	6	5	9	8	7
8	2	5	3	9	7	4	1	6
7	6	9	4	1	8	2	3	5

Mostly Odd-Even

4	1	7	9	2	8	5	6	3
2	8	3	5	6	7	4	9	1
5	9	6	4	3	1	2	7	8
3	2	9	7	8	5	6	1	4
8	4	1	2	9	6	3	5	7
6	7	5	1	4	3	9	8	2
1	3	2	8	5	9	7	4	6
7	5	4	6	1	2	8	3	9
9	6	8	3	7	4	1	2	5

Thermo 1

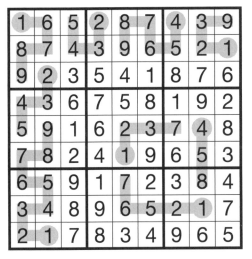

1	6	5	2	8	7	4	3	9
8	7	4	3	9	6	5	2	1
9	2	3	5	4	1	8	7	6
4	3	6	7	5	8	1	9	2
5	9	1	6	2	3	7	4	8
7	8	2	4	1	9	6	5	3
6	5	9	1	7	2	3	8	4
3	4	8	9	6	5	2	1	7
2	1	7	8	3	4	9	6	5

Thermo 2

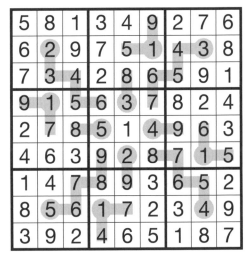

5	8	1	3	4	9	2	7	6
6	2	9	7	5	1	4	3	8
7	3	4	2	8	6	5	9	1
9	1	5	6	3	7	8	2	4
2	7	8	5	1	4	9	6	3
4	6	3	9	2	8	7	1	5
1	4	7	8	9	3	6	5	2
8	5	6	1	7	2	3	4	9
3	9	2	4	6	5	1	8	7

Thermo 3

9	5	1	6	4	2	7	8	3
7	6	2	8	5	3	4	9	1
8	3	4	7	9	1	5	6	2
4	1	3	2	6	5	9	7	8
5	9	8	3	7	4	2	1	6
2	7	6	1	8	9	3	4	5
3	2	9	4	1	6	8	5	7
1	8	5	9	2	7	6	3	4
6	4	7	5	3	8	1	2	9

Thermo 4

4	6	8	9	3	5	1	7	2
5	1	7	8	4	2	9	3	6
9	2	3	1	7	6	5	8	4
7	9	5	2	8	4	3	6	1
2	3	6	7	1	9	8	4	5
8	4	1	5	6	3	7	2	9
3	7	2	4	5	1	6	9	8
6	5	9	3	2	8	4	1	7
1	8	4	6	9	7	2	5	3

Thermo 5

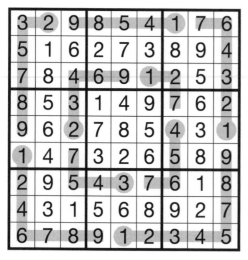

Thermo 6

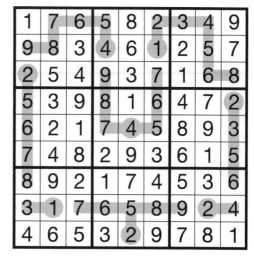

Thermo 7

Thermo 8

Invisibulls

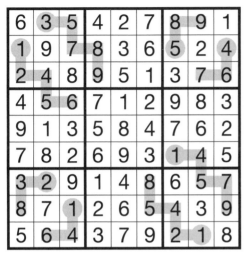

Broken Thermometer

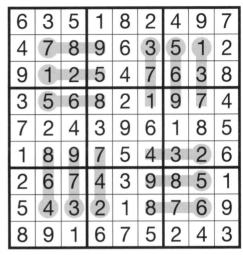

Killer 1

3	2	4	1	6	7	5	9	8
1	9	6	8	4	5	3	2	7
5	7	8	2	9	3	1	4	6
2	6	5	4	1	8	7	3	9
9	1	7	3	5	6	4	8	2
8	4	3	9	7	2	6	1	5
4	5	1	6	2	9	8	7	3
7	3	2	5	8	1	9	6	4
6	8	9	7	3	4	2	5	1

Killer 2

2	9	1	6	4	7	3	8	5
8	6	5	9	3	2	1	4	7
4	7	3	8	1	5	9	2	6
3	5	9	2	6	1	8	7	4
6	4	2	7	8	3	5	1	9
1	8	7	5	9	4	6	3	2
9	3	6	4	2	8	7	5	1
7	1	4	3	5	9	2	6	8
5	2	8	1	7	6	4	9	3

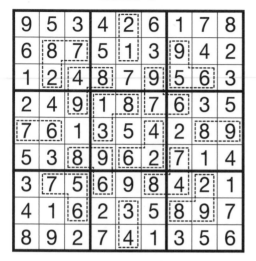

9	5	3	4	2	6	1	7	8
6	8	7	5	1	3	9	4	2
1	2	4	8	7	9	5	6	3
2	4	9	1	8	7	6	3	5
7	6	1	3	5	4	2	8	9
5	3	8	9	6	2	7	1	4
3	7	5	6	9	8	4	2	1
4	1	6	2	3	5	8	9	7
8	9	2	7	4	1	3	5	6

6	4	7	8	9	1	5	2	3
3	2	9	4	7	5	8	6	1
8	5	1	2	3	6	4	7	9
2	9	8	6	4	7	1	3	5
7	6	4	1	5	3	2	9	8
5	1	3	9	2	8	6	4	7
9	7	2	5	1	4	3	8	6
1	3	6	7	8	2	9	5	4
4	8	5	3	6	9	7	1	2

Killer 5

Killer 6

2	6	5	3	4	9	7	1	8
7	8	9	2	1	6	5	3	4
4	1	3	8	7	5	2	6	9
6	9	4	7	2	1	3	8	5
8	3	1	5	6	4	9	7	2
5	2	7	9	3	8	6	4	1
3	4	6	1	5	2	8	9	7
9	7	2	4	8	3	1	5	6
1	5	8	6	9	7	4	2	3

8	5	2	3	6	9	4	7	1
6	1	7	8	4	5	2	3	9
9	4	3	2	7	1	6	5	8
5	2	4	9	8	3	7	1	6
3	7	6	1	5	4	9	8	2
1	8	9	7	2	6	5	4	3
2	9	5	4	3	8	1	6	7
4	3	1	6	9	7	8	2	5
7	6	8	5	1	2	3	9	4

Killer 7

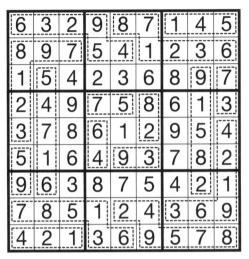

6	3	2	9	8	7	1	4	5
8	9	7	5	4	1	2	3	6
1	5	4	2	3	6	8	9	7
2	4	9	7	5	8	6	1	3
3	7	8	6	1	2	9	5	4
5	1	6	4	9	3	7	8	2
9	6	3	8	7	5	4	2	1
7	8	5	1	2	4	3	6	9
4	2	1	3	6	9	5	7	8

Killer 8

6	5	3	8	2	1	4	9	7
1	8	7	9	5	4	6	2	3
9	2	4	6	7	3	5	1	8
5	1	9	2	6	8	7	3	4
3	7	2	4	9	5	1	8	6
4	6	8	3	1	7	9	5	2
7	3	1	5	8	6	2	4	9
2	4	5	7	3	9	8	6	1
8	9	6	1	4	2	3	7	5

Killer Sums

8	9	7	1	5	6	2	3	4
4	3	1	7	2	9	6	8	5
6	2	5	4	8	3	1	7	9
1	8	2	6	9	7	4	5	3
3	7	9	5	4	1	8	2	6
5	4	6	8	3	2	7	9	1
9	5	8	2	6	4	3	1	7
7	6	3	9	1	8	5	4	2
2	1	4	3	7	5	9	6	8

Liar Killer

6	3	7	2	5	4	9	8	1
8	2	4	6	1	9	5	3	7
5	1	9	3	8	7	6	4	2
9	5	1	4	3	2	8	7	6
2	8	6	5	7	1	4	9	3
4	7	3	9	6	8	1	2	5
7	6	5	8	4	3	2	1	9
3	4	2	1	9	5	7	6	8
1	9	8	7	2	6	3	5	4

Clone 1

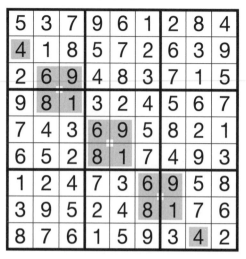

5	3	7	9	6	1	2	8	4
4	1	8	5	7	2	6	3	9
2	6	9	4	8	3	7	1	5
9	8	1	3	2	4	5	6	7
7	4	3	6	9	5	8	2	1
6	5	2	8	1	7	4	9	3
1	2	4	7	3	6	9	5	8
3	9	5	2	4	8	1	7	6
8	7	6	1	5	9	3	4	2

Clone 2

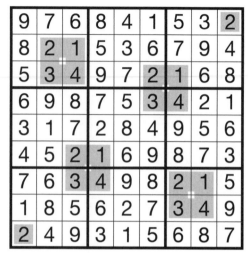

9	7	6	8	4	1	5	3	2
8	2	1	5	3	6	7	9	4
5	3	4	9	7	2	1	6	8
6	9	8	7	5	3	4	2	1
3	1	7	2	8	4	9	5	6
4	5	2	1	6	9	8	7	3
7	6	3	4	9	8	2	1	5
1	8	5	6	2	7	3	4	9
2	4	9	3	1	5	6	8	7

Clone 3

3	9	7	8	2	1	5	4	6
2	4	1	3	6	5	9	8	7
5	6	8	4	7	9	3	1	2
9	5	2	6	1	8	4	7	3
7	1	3	5	4	2	6	9	8
6	8	4	7	9	3	1	2	5
1	3	6	2	8	4	7	5	9
8	7	9	1	5	6	2	3	4
4	2	5	9	3	7	8	6	1

Clone 4

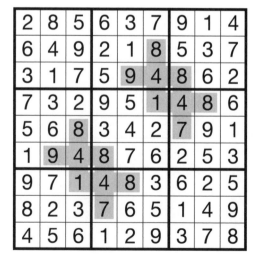

2	8	5	6	3	7	9	1	4
6	4	9	2	1	8	5	3	7
3	1	7	5	9	4	8	6	2
7	3	2	9	5	1	4	8	6
5	6	8	3	4	2	7	9	1
1	9	4	8	7	6	2	5	3
9	7	1	4	8	3	6	2	5
8	2	3	7	6	5	1	4	9
4	5	6	1	2	9	3	7	8

Clone 5

5	1	8	4	2	6	3	7	9
7	3	9	8	5	1	2	6	4
4	2	6	9	3	7	1	5	8
6	9	7	1	4	8	5	2	3
3	4	1	2	9	5	6	8	7
8	5	2	6	7	3	9	4	1
1	7	3	5	8	2	4	9	6
9	8	5	3	6	4	7	1	2
2	6	4	7	1	9	8	3	5

Clone 6

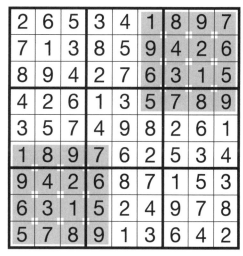

2	6	5	3	4	1	8	9	7
7	1	3	8	5	9	4	2	6
8	9	4	2	7	6	3	1	5
4	2	6	1	3	5	7	8	9
3	5	7	4	9	8	2	6	1
1	8	9	7	6	2	5	3	4
9	4	2	6	8	7	1	5	3
6	3	1	5	2	4	9	7	8
5	7	8	9	1	3	6	4	2

Clone 7

9	1	2	3	5	8	6	7	4
7	4	3	2	6	9	1	8	5
6	5	8	7	1	4	9	2	3
2	7	1	4	9	6	3	5	8
8	3	6	1	2	5	4	9	7
4	9	5	8	7	3	2	6	1
1	8	9	6	3	7	5	4	2
3	6	7	5	4	2	8	1	9
5	2	4	9	8	1	7	3	6

Clone 8

7	8	5	6	1	9	2	3	4
9	2	3	4	5	7	8	1	6
6	1	4	8	3	2	7	9	5
8	3	6	5	4	1	9	2	7
4	9	2	3	7	8	5	6	1
1	5	7	2	9	6	3	4	8
3	7	9	1	6	5	4	8	2
2	4	1	7	8	3	6	5	9
5	6	8	9	2	4	1	7	3

Invisible Clone

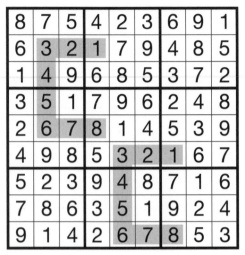

8	7	5	4	2	3	6	9	1
6	3	2	1	7	9	4	8	5
1	4	9	6	8	5	3	7	2
3	5	1	7	9	6	2	4	8
2	6	7	8	1	4	5	3	9
4	9	8	5	3	2	1	6	7
5	2	3	9	4	8	7	1	6
7	8	6	3	5	1	9	2	4
9	1	4	2	6	7	8	5	3

Liar Clone

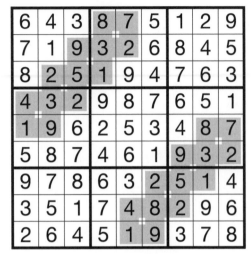

6	4	3	8	7	5	1	2	9
7	1	9	3	2	6	8	4	5
8	2	5	1	9	4	7	6	3
4	3	2	9	8	7	6	5	1
1	9	6	2	5	3	4	8	7
5	8	7	4	6	1	9	3	2
9	7	8	6	3	2	5	1	4
3	5	1	7	4	8	2	9	6
2	6	4	5	1	9	3	7	8

Consecutive Pairs 1

2	3	8	1	6	7	9	5	4
1	4	7	9	5	8	6	2	3
9	5	6	2	4	3	7	8	1
4	8	9	3	2	1	5	6	7
3	7	5	4	9	6	8	1	2
6	2	1	7	8	5	4	3	9
5	1	2	6	7	9	3	4	8
7	6	3	8	1	4	2	9	5
8	9	4	5	3	2	1	7	6

Consecutive Pairs 2

6	7	8	9	5	4	3	1	2
3	5	9	1	2	8	7	6	4
4	1	2	6	7	3	8	5	9
9	3	7	8	6	2	5	4	1
1	2	4	7	9	5	6	8	3
8	6	5	4	3	1	9	2	7
2	9	1	5	8	7	4	3	6
7	8	3	2	4	6	1	9	5
5	4	6	3	1	9	2	7	8

Consecutive Pairs 3

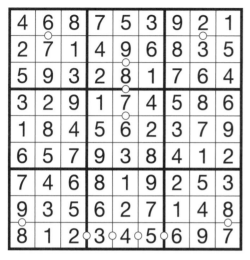

Consecutive Pairs 4

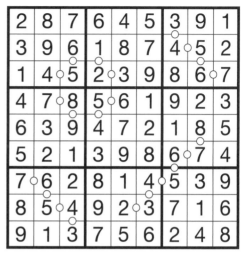

Consecutive Pairs 5

Consecutive Pairs 6

Consecutive Pairs 7

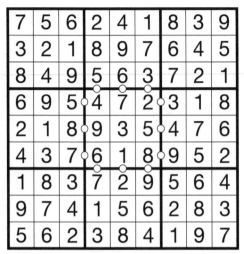

Consecutive Pairs 8

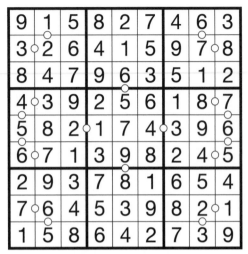

Greater Than Consecutive Pairs

9	8	4	5	1	7	6	3	2
1	6	5	2	3	4	8	9	7
3	2	7	6	8	9	4	1	5
8	5	3	7	6	1	2	4	9
2	7	1	4	9	8	5	6	3
4	9	6	3	5	2	1	7	8
5	4	8	9	7	6	3	2	1
6	1	9	8	2	3	7	5	4
7	3	2	1	4	5	9	8	6

Nonconsecutive Pairs

1	6	3	8	5	2	7	4	9
5	2	7	4	9	6	1	8	3
8	9	4	7	1	3	6	2	5
9	3	6	2	8	5	4	7	1
4	1	2	9	6	7	3	5	8
7	5	8	3	4	1	2	9	6
6	7	1	5	2	9	8	3	4
2	4	9	6	3	8	5	1	7
3	8	5	1	7	4	9	6	2

Zones 1

9	4	7	2	5	1	6	8	3
8	5	2	3	7	6	4	9	1
6	3	1	4	8	9	5	2	7
3	7	6	5	1	2	9	4	8
2	1	4	9	3	8	7	5	6
5	9	8	7	6	4	1	3	2
4	6	5	8	2	7	3	1	9
7	2	9	1	4	3	8	6	5
1	8	3	6	9	5	2	7	4

Zones 2

3	6	5	1	7	9	4	8	2
8	7	4	3	5	2	6	9	1
1	2	9	6	8	4	3	7	5
9	4	6	8	2	3	5	1	7
2	3	7	5	6	1	9	4	8
5	8	1	9	4	7	2	3	6
7	1	3	2	9	6	8	5	4
4	5	2	7	3	8	1	6	9
6	9	8	4	1	5	7	2	3

Zones 3

5	6	9	1	2	3	8	4	7
3	4	2	8	7	9	6	5	1
8	1	7	4	6	5	2	9	3
6	9	4	3	8	7	1	2	5
7	2	5	9	4	1	3	8	6
1	8	3	6	5	2	4	7	9
9	7	6	2	3	4	5	1	8
4	5	8	7	1	6	9	3	2
2	3	1	5	9	8	7	6	4

Zones 4

9	8	5	7	3	2	6	1	4
6	3	4	8	9	1	5	7	2
1	2	7	6	5	4	8	9	3
4	5	9	1	2	7	3	6	8
3	6	1	9	8	5	4	2	7
8	7	2	3	4	6	1	5	9
7	1	8	4	6	9	2	3	5
5	9	3	2	1	8	7	4	6
2	4	6	5	7	3	9	8	1

Zones 5

9	2	8	6	7	1	4	3	5
4	7	3	2	5	8	6	9	1
1	5	6	4	9	3	7	8	2
5	8	4	9	2	6	3	1	7
2	3	7	5	1	4	9	6	8
6	9	1	8	3	7	2	5	4
8	4	9	1	6	2	5	7	3
3	6	2	7	8	5	1	4	9
7	1	5	3	4	9	8	2	6

Zones 6

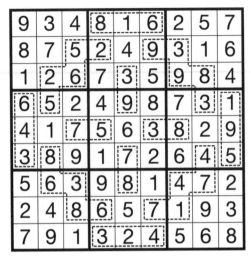

Zones 7

1	5	7	2	6	3	8	4	9
3	9	6	1	4	8	2	7	5
8	4	2	5	9	7	1	3	6
7	6	3	4	8	5	9	1	2
2	1	5	9	7	6	4	8	3
9	8	4	3	1	2	5	6	7
6	2	9	8	3	4	7	5	1
4	7	1	6	5	9	3	2	8
5	3	8	7	2	1	6	9	4

Zones 8

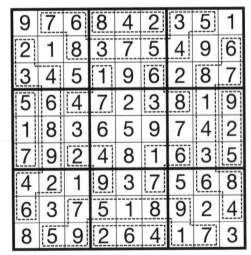

Liar Zones

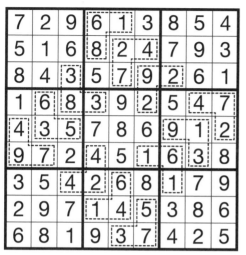

7	2	9	6	1	3	8	5	4
5	1	6	8	2	4	7	9	3
8	4	3	5	7	9	2	6	1
1	6	8	3	9	2	5	4	7
4	3	5	7	8	6	9	1	2
9	7	2	4	5	1	6	3	8
3	5	4	2	6	8	1	7	9
2	9	7	1	4	5	3	8	6
6	8	1	9	3	7	4	2	5

Pick One Zone

3	7	5	9	8	6	1	4	2
4	8	1	7	5	2	9	6	3
2	6	9	3	1	4	7	8	5
6	3	8	2	4	7	5	9	1
7	1	4	5	6	9	3	2	8
5	9	2	1	3	8	6	7	4
9	4	3	6	2	1	8	5	7
1	2	6	8	7	5	4	3	9
8	5	7	4	9	3	2	1	6

Renban Groups 1

4	8	7	6	2	1	3	9	5
5	6	1	4	3	9	8	7	2
3	9	2	8	5	7	4	6	1
7	1	9	2	8	4	6	5	3
8	5	3	7	1	6	2	4	9
2	4	6	5	9	3	7	1	8
1	3	4	9	7	2	5	8	6
9	7	5	3	6	8	1	2	4
6	2	8	1	4	5	9	3	7

Renban Groups 2

6	2	5	1	3	4	8	9	7
4	8	9	2	6	7	3	5	1
3	7	1	5	8	9	6	4	2
1	5	3	4	9	8	7	2	6
2	9	6	3	7	1	4	8	5
7	4	8	6	5	2	1	3	9
5	1	4	7	2	3	9	6	8
9	3	2	8	1	6	5	7	4
8	6	7	9	4	5	2	1	3

Renban Groups 3

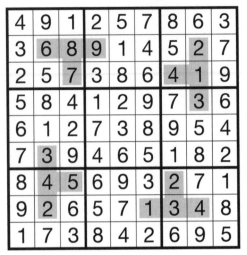

4	9	1	2	5	7	8	6	3
3	6	8	9	1	4	5	2	7
2	5	7	3	8	6	4	1	9
5	8	4	1	2	9	7	3	6
6	1	2	7	3	8	9	5	4
7	3	9	4	6	5	1	8	2
8	4	5	6	9	3	2	7	1
9	2	6	5	7	1	3	4	8
1	7	3	8	4	2	6	9	5

Renban Groups 4

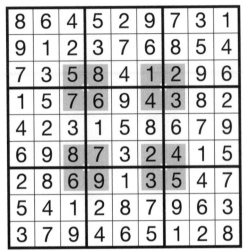

8	6	4	5	2	9	7	3	1
9	1	2	3	7	6	8	5	4
7	3	5	8	4	1	2	9	6
1	5	7	6	9	4	3	8	2
4	2	3	1	5	8	6	7	9
6	9	8	7	3	2	4	1	5
2	8	6	9	1	3	5	4	7
5	4	1	2	8	7	9	6	3
3	7	9	4	6	5	1	2	8

Renban Groups 5

6	4	2	7	1	5	8	9	3
5	1	8	3	6	9	2	7	4
3	9	7	4	8	2	1	6	5
7	3	5	6	4	1	9	8	2
1	2	9	5	3	8	6	4	7
8	6	4	2	9	7	5	3	1
4	5	3	8	2	6	7	1	9
9	7	6	1	5	4	3	2	8
2	8	1	9	7	3	4	5	6

Renban Groups 6

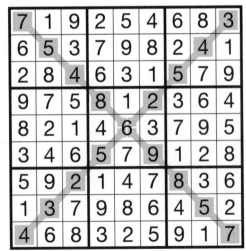

7	1	9	2	5	4	6	8	3
6	5	3	7	9	8	2	4	1
2	8	4	6	3	1	5	7	9
9	7	5	8	1	2	3	6	4
8	2	1	4	6	3	7	9	5
3	4	6	5	7	9	1	2	8
5	9	2	1	4	7	8	3	6
1	3	7	9	8	6	4	5	2
4	6	8	3	2	5	9	1	7

Renban Groups 7

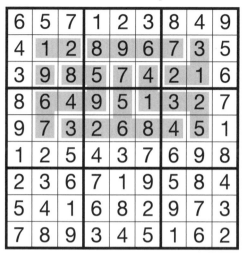

6	5	7	1	2	3	8	4	9
4	1	2	8	9	6	7	3	5
3	9	8	5	7	4	2	1	6
8	6	4	9	5	1	3	2	7
9	7	3	2	6	8	4	5	1
1	2	5	4	3	7	6	9	8
2	3	6	7	1	9	5	8	4
5	4	1	6	8	2	9	7	3
7	8	9	3	4	5	1	6	2

Renban Groups 8

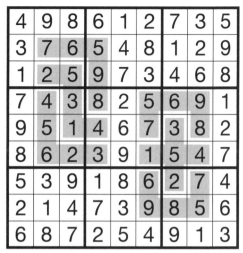

4	9	8	6	1	2	7	3	5
3	7	6	5	4	8	1	2	9
1	2	5	9	7	3	4	6	8
7	4	3	8	2	5	6	9	1
9	5	1	4	6	7	3	8	2
8	6	2	3	9	1	5	4	7
5	3	9	1	8	6	2	7	4
2	1	4	7	3	9	8	5	6
6	8	7	2	5	4	9	1	3

Anti-Renban Groups

4	5	6	9	1	8	2	7	3
3	7	9	5	6	2	1	4	8
8	1	2	7	3	4	6	5	9
5	6	8	1	2	3	7	9	4
9	2	7	4	5	6	3	8	1
1	4	3	8	7	9	5	6	2
2	8	1	6	4	5	9	3	7
6	3	4	2	9	7	8	1	5
7	9	5	3	8	1	4	2	6

Unique Renban Groups

9	5	1	3	6	4	8	2	7
4	7	3	2	8	5	6	9	1
8	6	2	7	9	1	5	3	4
5	1	4	8	3	2	9	7	6
6	2	8	9	5	7	4	1	3
3	9	7	1	4	6	2	8	5
7	4	9	5	1	8	3	6	2
2	8	5	6	7	3	1	4	9
1	3	6	4	2	9	7	5	8

Extra Regions or Clones?

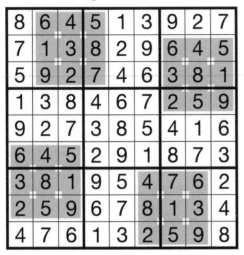

8	6	4	5	1	3	9	2	7
7	1	3	8	2	9	6	4	5
5	9	2	7	4	6	3	8	1
1	3	8	4	6	7	2	5	9
9	2	7	3	8	5	4	1	6
6	4	5	2	9	1	8	7	3
3	8	1	9	5	4	7	6	2
2	5	9	6	7	8	1	3	4
4	7	6	1	3	2	5	9	8

Renban Groups/Extra Regions

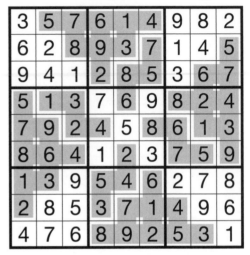

3	5	7	6	1	4	9	8	2
6	2	8	9	3	7	1	4	5
9	4	1	2	8	5	3	6	7
5	1	3	7	6	9	8	2	4
7	9	2	4	5	8	6	1	3
8	6	4	1	2	3	7	5	9
1	3	9	5	4	6	2	7	8
2	8	5	3	7	1	4	9	6
4	7	6	8	9	2	5	3	1

Extra Regions/Odd-Even

9	5	3	4	7	1	6	8	2
8	4	1	5	6	2	7	3	9
6	2	7	3	9	8	4	5	1
1	7	4	9	5	3	2	6	8
5	8	9	6	2	7	1	4	3
2	3	6	1	8	4	9	7	5
4	9	8	2	3	6	5	1	7
3	1	2	7	4	5	8	9	6
7	6	5	8	1	9	3	2	4

Consecutive Pairs/Renban Groups

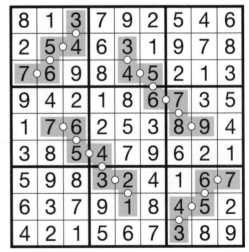

8	1	3	7	9	2	5	4	6
2	5	4	6	3	1	9	7	8
7	6	9	8	4	5	2	1	3
9	4	2	1	8	6	7	3	5
1	7	6	2	5	3	8	9	4
3	8	5	4	7	9	6	2	1
5	9	8	3	2	4	1	6	7
6	3	7	9	1	8	4	5	2
4	2	1	5	6	7	3	8	9

Thermo Killer

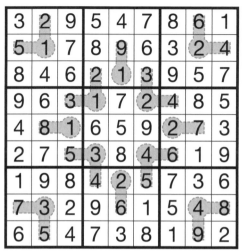

Clone/Zones

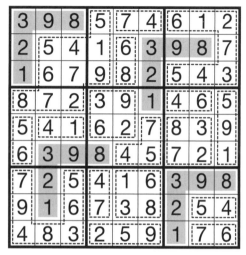

Renban Groups/Killer

1	4	2	3	6	9	8	7	5
6	5	9	4	8	7	1	2	3
8	7	3	1	2	5	6	9	4
7	1	6	5	9	3	4	8	2
9	2	8	6	7	4	5	3	1
4	3	5	2	1	8	9	6	7
3	9	1	7	5	6	2	4	8
2	8	4	9	3	1	7	5	6
5	6	7	8	4	2	3	1	9

Consecutive Pairs/Odd-Even

8	4	3	2	9	6	1	7	5
7	1	9	3	4	5	8	6	2
6	5	2	1	8	7	4	9	3
5	6	7	8	1	9	2	3	4
9	8	4	7	2	3	5	1	6
3	2	1	5	6	4	7	8	9
2	7	6	9	5	1	3	4	8
1	9	8	4	3	2	6	5	7
4	3	5	6	7	8	9	2	1

Zones or Killer?

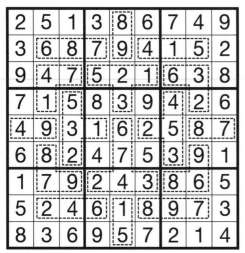

2	5	1	3	8	6	7	4	9
3	6	8	7	9	4	1	5	2
9	4	7	5	2	1	6	3	8
7	1	5	8	3	9	4	2	6
4	9	3	1	6	2	5	8	7
6	8	2	4	7	5	3	9	1
1	7	9	2	4	3	8	6	5
5	2	4	6	1	8	9	7	3
8	3	6	9	5	7	2	1	4

Odd-Even/Killer

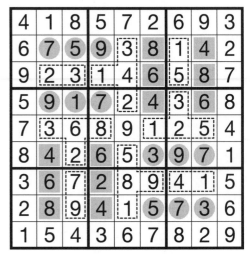

4	1	8	5	7	2	6	9	3
6	7	5	9	3	8	1	4	2
9	2	3	1	4	6	5	8	7
5	9	1	7	2	4	3	6	8
7	3	6	8	9	1	2	5	4
8	4	2	6	5	3	9	7	1
3	6	7	2	8	9	4	1	5
2	8	9	4	1	5	7	3	6
1	5	4	3	6	7	8	2	9

Cloned Thermometers

3	6	7	2	1	8	9	5	4
2	4	5	9	7	6	8	3	1
1	8	9	3	5	4	7	6	2
4	3	6	1	2	9	5	8	7
7	1	8	5	6	3	4	2	9
9	5	2	4	8	7	6	1	3
6	9	1	7	3	5	2	4	8
5	2	4	8	9	1	3	7	6
8	7	3	6	4	2	1	9	5

All in One

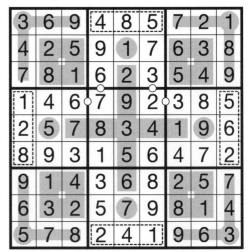

3	6	9	4	8	5	7	2	1
4	2	5	9	1	7	6	3	8
7	8	1	6	2	3	5	4	9
1	4	6	7	9	2	3	8	5
2	5	7	8	3	4	1	9	6
8	9	3	1	5	6	4	7	2
9	1	4	3	6	8	2	5	7
6	3	2	5	7	9	8	1	4
5	7	8	2	4	1	9	6	3